Golda Meir

with profiles of
David Ben-Gurion
and Yitzhak Rabin

World Book, Inc.
a Scott Fetzer company
Chicago

BIOGRAPHICAL ⊕ CONNECTIONS

Writer: Lori Meek Schuldt.

© 2007 World Book, Inc. All rights reserved. The content of this publication may not be reproduced in whole or in part in any form without prior written permission from the publisher. WORLD BOOK and the GLOBE DEVICE are registered trademarks or trademarks of World Book, Inc.

World Book, Inc.
233 N. Michigan Ave.
Chicago, IL 60601

For information about other World Book publications, visit our Web site at **www.worldbook.com** or call 1-800-WORLDBK (967-5325).
For information about sales to schools and libraries, call **1-800-975-3250 (United States)**, or **1-800-837-5365 (Canada)**.

Library of Congress Cataloging-in-Publication Data

Schuldt, Lori Meek.
  Golda Meir: with profiles of David Ben-Gurion and Yitzhak Rabin /
[writer, Lori Meek Schuldt].
    p. cm. -- (Biographical connections)
  Summary: "A biography of Golda Meir, with profiles of two prominent individuals, who are associated through the influences they had on one another, the successes they achieved, or the goals they worked toward. Includes recommended readings and web sites"--Provided by publisher.
  Includes bibliographical references and index.
  ISBN-13: 978-0-7166-1829-4
  ISBN-10: 0-7166-1829-X
  1. Meir, Golda, 1898-1978--Juvenile literature. 2. Women prime ministers-—Israel--Biography--Juvenile literature. 3. Prime ministers--Israel--Biography--Juvenile literature. 4. Ben-Gurion, David, 1886-1973--Juvenile literature. 5. Rabin, Yitzhak, 1922-1995--Juvenile literature. I. World Book, Inc. II. Title. III. Series.
DS126.6.M42S38 2007
956.9405'3092--dc22
[B]
                        2006017513

Printed in the United States of America
1 2 3 4 5 10 09 08 07 06

Contents

Acknowledgments

The publisher gratefully acknowledges the following sources for the photographs in this volume. All maps are the exclusive property of World Book, Inc.

Cover	© Corbis/Bettmann
	© John Phillips, Time Life Pictures/Getty Images
	© William Karel, Sygma/Corbis
7	© John Phillips, Time Life Pictures/Getty Images
13	© Keystone/Getty Images
16	© Corbis/Bettmann
21	© Topham/The Image Works
22-25	© Micha Bar-Am, Magnum Photos
27	© David Rubinger, Time Life Pictures/Getty Images
28	WORLD BOOK map
31-41	University of Wisconsin-Milwaukee, Archives
47	© Bar-Am Collection/Magnum Photos
60	© Dmitri Kessel, Time Life Pictures/Getty Images
65	© Bar-Am Collection/Magnum Photos
67	University of Wisconsin-Milwaukee, Archives
69	© Corbis/Bettmann
72	© AFP/Getty Images
75	AP/Wide World
76-79	© David Rubinger, Corbis
80	University of Wisconsin-Milwaukee, Archives
81-82	© Corbis/Bettmann
85	© Micha Bar-Am, Magnum Photos
87	© AFP/Getty Images
88	© Keystone/Getty Images
89	© William Karel, Sygma/Corbis
93	© Moshe Milner, Sygma/Corbis
97	© Micha Bar-Am, Magnum Photos
100	© *Evening Standard*/Getty Images
103	© Micha Bar-Am, Magnum Photos
105-107	AP/Wide World

Preface

Biographical Connections takes a contextual approach in presenting the lives of important people. In each volume, there is a biography of a central figure. This biography is preceded and followed by profiles of other individuals whose lifework connects in some way to that of the central figure. The three subjects are associated through the influences they had on one another, the successes they achieved, or the goals they worked toward. The series includes men and women from around the world and throughout history in a variety of fields.

This volume presents three people who made significant contributions to the development of Israel, a modern nation established in an ancient land. Among their many accomplishments, each of them served as prime minister, the head of Israel's government. David Ben-Gurion, the subject of the opening profile, was Israel's first prime minister. He served from 1948, when the nation of Israel officially came into being, until 1953 and from 1955 to 1963. Golda Meir, the central biography in this volume, was prime minister from 1969 to 1974. Yitzhak Rabin, the subject of the concluding biography, was prime minister from 1974 to 1977 and from 1992 until his assassination in 1995. In addition to feeling pride as leader of Israel's people, each of these three individuals felt a special connection to the land itself. All three spent time early in their careers on communal farm settlements in the nation now known as Israel called *kibbutzim*. Many of these settlements were in sparsely populated areas where the work involved hard labor clearing rocks and draining mosquito-ridden swamps to make the soil suitable for agriculture. Ironically, each of the three leaders initially expected to live out his or her life in contentment on a kibbutz, yet each was destined for a larger role in Israel's history.

Ben-Gurion was among the Jewish pioneers who left the Russian-ruled part of Europe in the early 1900's to settle in the southwestern Asian region, where the religious and cultural identity of the Jews began to develop as early as 1800 B.C. Most of the Jews were driven out of that region in the A.D. 130's by the Romans, who called the region *Palaestina*, a name that became *Palestine* in English. During the A.D. 600's, Muslim Arabs took control of Palestine and eventually made up most of the region's population. When Ben-Gurion arrived in 1906, Palestine was under Turkish rule as part of the Ottoman Empire. The Jewish pioneers called themselves *Zionists,* because in Hebrew, the language of the Jewish people, the name for Palestine is *Zion.* The Zionists sought to build the new Jewish nation with their own hands and established the first kibbutzim. Ben-Gurion helped form an armed guard unit to defend Jewish settlements against Arab opponents. In the 1920's, he helped create a labor federation to unite various organizations of pioneers, farmers, and workers. In the 1930's, he oversaw the agency that directed Jewish affairs in Palestine until the independent State of Israel came into existence with a proclamation he publicly read.

Golda Meir also grew up in Russian-ruled Europe, but as a child moved to the United States with her family. By the time Meir emigrated to Palestine in 1921, it had been taken over by the British. Meir first lived on a kibbutz but soon became an activist in the growing labor movement. An engaging and persuasive public speaker, Meir spent much of her time in the 1930's traveling abroad to raise money for Zionism. Fluent in English, she made many subsequent successful appeals to the Jewish community of the United States, particularly for the financing that was vital to the new nation's early survival against Arab attacks following Israel's proclamation of independence. Meir served as minister of labor and minister of foreign affairs in the 1950's and 1960's before becoming prime minister.

Yitzhak Rabin was born in Jerusalem the year after Meir arrived in Palestine. His parents were Zionist pioneers who crossed paths with both Ben-Gurion and Meir. Rabin was a soldier in the 1940's. He fought for the establishment of an independent Jewish state, and he smuggled Jewish refugees from Nazi Germany into Palestine in defiance of British immigration restrictions. He continued his military career after Israel came into existence, defending the new country against Arab opposition. As head of the Israel Defense Forces, he planned the strategy for Israel's spectacular victory against Arab forces in 1967 that made him a national hero. Soon afterward, he embarked on the political career that would lead him to the nation's top office, where he would emerge as a strong leader for peace in the region. ■

David Ben-Gurion (1886–1973)

David Ben-Gurion *(behn GOO rih uhn)* devoted his life to the establishment and maintenance of the Jewish homeland that came into existence in 1948 as the nation of Israel. He often is referred to as the founder of Israel, and he served as the nation's first president. His keen mind and forceful personality made him a world leader respected by allies and enemies alike.

JEWISH IDENTITY

Jewish identity is based on a combination of religious, historical, and ethnic factors. According to Jewish law, any person born to a Jewish mother or converted to *Judaism,* the religion of the Jews, is considered a Jew. The Jews trace their ancestry to a shepherd named Abraham, who settled with his family in the region of Canaan—an area north of Egypt between the Mediterranean Sea and the Jordan River—sometime between 1800 and 1500 B.C. The descendants of the 12 children of Abraham's grandson Jacob, who was also known as Israel, called themselves the *Twelve Tribes of Israel,* or Israelites. About 1000 B.C., the Israelite king David united the people of the region and founded the Kingdom of Israel. He made Jerusalem its capital. In the early 900's B.C., the 10 northern tribes split off from the 2 southern tribes. The northern kingdom continued to be called Israel. The southern kingdom was called Judah and kept Jerusalem as its capital. The word *Jew* comes from the name *Judah.* In the early 700's B.C., the Assyrians conquered Israel, which then ceased to exist as a nation. Its people scattered to other lands and lost their identity. In the late 580's B.C., the Babylonians conquered Judah, destroyed the Jews' temple, and took many Jews to Babylonia as prisoners. However, the people of Judah retained their Jewish identity even in exile. After the Persian king Cyrus conquered Babylonia in 539 B.C., he allowed the exiled Jews to resettle in Jerusalem and rebuild their temple. Some Jews remained in Babylonia. Later, the communities of Jews living outside the original Kingdom of Israel became known as the *Diaspora*. In 168 or 167 B.C., the descendants of the resettled Jews reestablished an independent kingdom called Judah. Roman troops invaded Judah, which they called *Judea*, in 63 B.C. and took control of the area. The Romans drove the Jews out of Jerusalem in A.D. 135. About this time, they gave the area the name *Palaestina*, which became *Palestine* in English. Over the centuries, control of Palestine changed hands a number of times as various groups invaded the region. In 1516, Palestine became part of the Ottoman Empire.

Throughout their history, Jews of the Diaspora suffered from religious persecution. But by the late 1800's, many people in Europe had begun to discriminate against Jews on ethnic rather than religious grounds. Prejudice against Jews became known as *anti-Semitism*—a term that is misleading because the root word *Semite* properly refers to all people who speak Semitic languages, not just Jews but also Arabs and some other non-Jewish peoples. Organized massacres called *pogroms (poh GROMZ or POH gruhmz)* raged throughout Russia and Poland in the late 1800's and early 1900's, prompting many Jews to look for ways to escape from such persecution. In 1882, groups of Jewish youths in Russia calling themselves *Hoveve-Zion* (Lovers of Zion) formed a movement to promote the establishment of Jewish settlements in Palestine. *Zion* is the poetic Hebrew name for Palestine. David Ben-Gurion's father was a Hoveve-Zion leader whose Zionist zeal was based more on the exciting notion of reestablishing a Jewish homeland than a fear of pogroms—from which the family's hometown was remarkably spared.

AN EARLY INTRODUCTION TO ZIONISM

David Ben-Gurion was born David Green (sometimes spelled Gruen) in Płońsk, Russia (now in Poland) on Oct. 16, 1886. His father, Avigdor Gruen, was a legal counselor and a leader in the local Jewish community. His mother, Sheindal Broitman Gruen, bore 11 children, but 6 of them died shortly after birth. David was the fourth of those who survived. He was a short, thin, sickly child, but he was nevertheless a clever boy. His devoutly religious mother affectionately called him "Duvcheh" and had aspirations for his becoming a rabbi someday. When David was 3 years old, his grandfather, Zvi Aryeh Green, started teaching him Hebrew, the biblical language of the Jewish people. The family spoke *Yiddish* at home. (Yiddish is the language of European Jews, which developed from a dialect of German. Yiddish contains many Hebrew and Slavic words and is written in Hebrew characters.) David also began to learn Russian once he started school. In Płońsk, groups of Russians, Poles, and Jews lived apart from one another but—unlike in many other parts of Eastern Europe at that time—coexisted peacefully. Young David grew up with a strong sense of pride in his Jewish heritage that the surrounding community did not discourage.

At the age of 5, David began attending a traditional Jewish religious school called a *heder,* where he studied Hebrew and the Bible. He also attended a Russian state school, where he studied Russian language and literature. An avid reader, David particularly enjoyed the works of the great Russian writers Leo Tolstoy and Fyodor Dostoevsky. David's father supplemented the boy's education with evening lectures on geography and history. When David was about 9 years old, he read two books that made a lifelong impression on him. The first, the Hebrew novel *Ahavatzion (The Love of Zion,* 1853) by Abraham Mapu, described people and events in biblical times in such a way that the ancient stories came to life in David's mind, reinforcing the Zionism he already felt through the teachings of his father and grandfather. The second book, a Russian translation of the American antislavery novel *Uncle Tom's Cabin* (1851–1852) by Harriet Beecher Stowe, filled David with revulsion at the idea of slavery and admiration for the slave Tom's "innate nobility."[1] David saw parallels between this story and the biblical story of Moses, who led the Israelites out of slavery to their homeland in Canaan.

When David was 11 years old, his mother died in childbirth. The already introverted boy became more withdrawn for several years as he worked through his deep grief over this loss. He approached his studies with little enthusiasm. After his father remarried, David ignored his stepmother. But the boy never lost his early interest in Zionism. One day, Płońsk was honored with a visit from Theodor Herzl, an Austrian journalist and playwright who was the chief leader of the Zionist movement. Herzl's then recently published book *The Jewish State* (1896) attracted many people to the Zionist cause, and he was greeted in Płońsk as the *Messiah*—that is, the anointed leader and liberator of the Jews. Ben-Gurion recalled in his memoirs: "He was a tall, finely featured man whose impressive black beard flowed wide down to his chest. One glimpse of him and I was ready to follow him then and there to the land of my ancestors. . . . Herzl was indeed like a Messiah since he galvanized the feeling of the youth that Eretz Israel [the Land of Israel] was achievable. He added, however, that it could only come to pass if we built it with our own hands."[2]

In 1900, at the age of 14, David and his friends Shmuel Fuchs and Shlomo Zemach established the Ezra Society to teach Hebrew to poor children in Płońsk's Jewish community. They started with about 150 boys, but many of their first pupils in turn taught the language to others, including some of the parents who had not learned it earlier. Within months, nearly everyone in the Jewish community could speak Hebrew. In late 1903, the three Ezra Society founders were disappointed to read in the newspaper about a recommendation that Herzl had made at the Zionist Congress in Basel, Switzerland. Herzl had proposed accepting an offer from the United Kingdom for the establishment of a Jewish state in Uganda, which was at that time a British protectorate, as a temporary refuge for European Jews while plans continued for the permanent settlement in Palestine. The trio of friends decided that the best way to reject such a stopgap measure was to emigrate to Palestine themselves to help speed up the process of reestablishing the Jewish homeland there. David would leave last, and Shlomo Zemach, who was a few years older than David, would eventually leave for Palestine on Dec. 13, 1904.

Ben-Gurion would later explain in a letter to his father that "settling the land is the only true Zionism, and all the rest is self-deception, empty talk, and a sheer waste of time."[3]

In the fall of 1904, David went to Warsaw, Poland (then under Russian control), about 40 miles (64 kilometers) southeast of Płońsk, to prepare for the entrance examination to a technical college there. He wanted to earn an engineering degree before departing for Palestine so that he would be well qualified as a builder. However, because of Russian restrictions against Jews, he could not get into a Russian high school to earn the diploma required for admittance to the technical school. In mid-1905, David joined the new Jewish workers' movement *Poalei Zion* (Workers for Zion). He returned to Płońsk, sporting a peasant blouse like those worn by Russian revolutionaries who were leading protests against the ruling *czar* (emperor), and became increasingly active in Poaeli Zion.

Zemach, now in Palestine, wrote long letters to David about his rigorous but satisfying life there. Inspired by these letters, David earned a reputation as a persuasive Zionist orator and a skilled debater. He organized strikes by the tailors and rope makers of Płońsk for better working conditions. The Poaeli Zion leaders in Warsaw sent him throughout the surrounding area to promote the movement. Seemingly rebellious with his Russian-style blouse, mustache, and long, curly hair, David also attracted the suspicion of the Warsaw police, who twice threw him in jail for subversive activity. Through a combination of legal skill, bribery, and luck, his father both times managed his release.

RELOCATION TO PALESTINE

In the summer of 1906, David set out with a group of Zionists from Płońsk on the long journey to Palestine. Among his traveling companions were Zemach, who had returned for a visit, and Rachel Nelkin, a young woman whom David had known since childhood. As young adults, David and Nelkin had become reacquainted and fallen in love. The travelers went by train to the seaport city of Odessa, Russia (now in Ukraine), where they boarded a dilapidated Russian freighter bound for Palestine. Traveling cheaply as fourth-class passengers, they slept on the hard floor of the ship's deck for the duration of the 14-day voyage. On the last night, David and Zemach stood at the railing for hours and watched as the shore of Palestine came into view with the morning light. The ship docked on Sept. 7, 1906, at the Palestinian port city of Jaffa, where David at last fulfilled his dream "to step onto the soil of the homeland."[4]

As soon as he stepped off the ship that morning, David was accosted by a group of Marxist activists hoping to recruit him for their organization. David, however, eager to build Eretz Israel, was not interested in discussing their political theories with them and quickly moved on. Jaffa was a shabby town bustling with political and mercantile activity—not exactly the rugged but pastoral environment he expected to find. He set off that afternoon with Rachel Nelkin, Shlomo Zemach, and about a dozen other young people. They walked about three hours northward to the Jewish farming settlement of Petah Tikvah, where they bought a meal and then slept in a farm field their first night in Palestine. David and Zemach subsequently rented a room together at the settlement. They and the others sought work as day laborers in the orange groves of Petah Tikvah. Because David was small and frail-looking compared with the indigenous Arab workers and the previously assimilated Jewish pioneers in the labor pool, he often was passed over for work and went hungry. He sometimes wandered to other nearby settlements looking for work. With the onset of winter, he suffered a series of bouts with malaria that the local doctor feared would kill him. But David persevered. Within a year, he grew stronger, and the malaria attacks subsided.

The immigrants from Płońsk earned a reputation as a hard-working group of people—or at least most of them did. The physical labor proved to be too strenuous for Nelkin, and she was fired from her first job in the orange groves. Others from Płońsk condemned her for detracting from their stalwart reputation. David not only failed to defend her from these critics but even agreed with them, placing his Zionist pride ahead of his personal loyalty. Their relationship was never the same afterward, and Nelkin soon fell in love with someone else whom she married a year later. David was heartbroken.

At the first conference of the Poalei Zion political party in Palestine after David's arrival in 1906, he was elected to both its central committee and the committee that drew up its program. Through Poalei Zion, David met Izhak Ben-Zvi, a fellow émigré from Russia who would become a lifelong friend and political associate. David lobbied for the adoption of Hebrew as the official language to be used by the party, as he believed it should be for the Land of Israel they would work to establish, but others were not as enthusiastic about the idea. In 1907, David and Ben-Zvi joined a group of Jewish pioneer farmers at the Sejera settlement in the remote Galilee region of northern Palestine. There David happily worked the land with a plow pulled by two oxen. However, Palestinian Arabs who inhabited the sparsely populated region regarded the Jewish newcomers as intruders in their territory, and they occasionally raided or attacked the settlement. David served in an armed guard unit—the first Jewish military force—called the *Hashomer* (The Watchmen) to defend Sejera. In the spring of 1909, after an Arab attacker died from wounds inflicted by a Jewish defender during a skirmish following an Arab ambush of Jews on the road, the Arabs avenged the death by killing a Jewish field guard at the settlement. Ben-Gurion recalled in his memoir: "It was then I realized the wider implications of this small clash. Sooner or later, Jews and Arabs would fight over this land."[5]

David left Sejera in the fall of 1909 and relocated to the Zichron Ya'akov settlement. He continued to work in the fields during the day but devoted many of his evenings to academic studies that would prepare him for university entrance examinations. He hoped to earn a law degree and then later win election to the parliament of the Ottoman Empire that governed Palestine. He also began to study French and Arabic.

A young David Green is shown in this photograph taken around 1908.

In 1910, David received word from Ben-Zvi that Poalei Zion had chosen David to join the editorial staff of the new party newspaper *Ahdut* (*Unity*) in Jerusalem. His articles for the Hebrew-language paper's first issue ran unsigned. In the second issue, however, he added the by-line *David Ben-Gurion,* using the Hebraized last name "in homage to a Jewish hero called Ben-Gurion who died defending Jerusalem against the final siege of the Roman legions in [A.D.] 70."[6] He kept the name for the rest of his life.

In November 1911, Ben-Gurion arrived in what is now Turkey and studied the Turkish language with a private tutor for several months as he prepared for the June 1912 entrance examinations to the University of Constantinople (now Istanbul University). Ben-Zvi helped him obtain a forged Russian high school diploma, and Ben-Gurion passed the examinations. He was admitted to the university in August. He earned a law degree with highest honors in the spring of 1914. On July 28, Ben-Gurion set sail for Palestine to take a vacation before starting his new career in law and politics. But his career plans changed abruptly. That day, Austria-Hungary declared war on Serbia, and suddenly World War I (1914–1918) was underway. Within a week, Germany joined Austria-Hungary in a military alliance that became known as the Central Powers, while Russia, France, and the British Empire backed Serbia as leaders of the Allies.

The Ottoman Empire officially entered the war on Oct. 31, 1914, on the side of the Central Powers. The Ottoman government began to impose restrictions on Jews, and it shut down the Poalei Zion newspaper *Ahdut.* Fearing that the Zionists might choose to support the Allies, the Ottomans arrested and deported many of the movement's leaders, including Ben-Gurion and Ben-Zvi, who in the spring of 1915 were placed on a Greek boat bound for the United States. During the month-long voyage across stormy seas, Ben-Gurion taught himself English. He also read passages from the works of the influential German philosopher G. W. F. Hegel, whose writings emphasized the importance of understanding human history in order to understand other aspects of human culture. Upon their arrival in New York City, Ben-Gurion and Ben-Zvi were welcomed by members of the American Poalei Zion group, and they began campaigning throughout the country for the Zionist cause. They also helped write the book *Yizkor* (*Commemoration*) about the early Hashomer. Ben-Gurion and Ben-Zvi also collaborated on the volume *Eretz Israel*, for which Ben-Gurion spent many long hours researching at the New York Public Library during 1916 and 1917.

In 1916, Ben-Gurion met a Russian-born nurse named Pauline "Paula" Munweiss at the home of a mutual acquaintance. Her carefree, fun-loving attitude was the opposite of Ben-Gurion's pensive, introverted personality, but the opposites attracted. Munweiss was an admirer of the exiled Russian socialist revolutionary Leon Trotsky, who was living in New York City at the time, and she was impressed with Ben-Gurion's articulate expression of his own political ideals. She offered to help him with his book research at the library, and they gradually fell in love. Ben-Gurion proposed marriage in late 1917, but his proposal was conditional upon her willingness to give up the modern conveniences of the United States for a lifetime of challenges in Palestine. She accepted, and they wed on Dec. 5, 1917, in a brief civil ceremony at city hall. Shortly afterward, they moved into an apartment in the New York City borough of Brooklyn.

A JEWISH NATIONAL HOME

On Nov. 2, 1917, in an attempt to gain Jewish support for their wartime effort to take control of Palestine, the British issued the Balfour Declaration. This document declared the British government in favor of the establishment of a Jewish national home in Palestine, without violating the civil and religious rights of the existing non-Jewish communities. Many Zionists believed the Balfour Declaration pledged British support for their goal of establishing a Jewish national state in Palestine. On April 26, 1918, Ben-Gurion signed up for the Jewish Legion, a division of the British Army composed of Jewish volunteer soldiers, many of whom were also exiles from Palestine. They wore standard British Army uniforms with the Star of David (also called *Shield of David*, from the Hebrew term *Magen David*) insignia on the sleeve. Ben-Gurion's battalion, officially called the 39th Battalion of the Royal Fusiliers,

During World War I, Ben-Gurion signed up for the Jewish Legion, a division of the British Army composed of Jewish volunteer soldiers.

trained in Windsor, Ontario, Canada. Ben-Gurion's leadership abilities became apparent to his commanding officers almost immediately, and he was promoted to corporal within a month of his enlistment.

On July 11, 1918, the 39th Battalion departed from Canada in a convoy of ships, stopping in England for about a month and then setting up camp in Egypt in preparation for advancement into Palestine. Shortly after arriving in Egypt, Ben-Gurion suffered an attack of *dysentery* (a disease of the intestines caused by microscopic organisms) and was hospitalized for several weeks in Cairo. While recovering there in September 1918, he received word that back in New York City, his wife had given birth to their first child, a daughter to whom they gave the Hebrew name *Ge'ula,* meaning *redemption.* Meanwhile, in the war, the fighting was winding down. Before Ben-Gurion's battalion reached Palestine, the British gained control. On Oct. 30, the Ottoman Empire signed an armistice to end its participation in the war. World War I ended on Nov. 11, 1918, with the signing of an armistice by Germany, the last of the Central Powers to surrender. By mid-December, Ben-Gurion was back in Palestine.

By 1919, Ben-Gurion was a Zionist leader in Palestine. His wife and daughter arrived at Jaffa on Nov. 15, 1919. The separation had been particularly hard on Paula, who respected her husband's Zionist ideals but did not share his passion for them and thus had felt the loss of companionship more personally. She was glad to be reunited with him at last. Ben-Gurion was discharged from the army shortly after his family arrived. The couple's second child, a son named Amos, was born in the late summer of 1920.

The League of Nations, an international association of countries created to maintain peace among the world's nations, was established in January 1920. Under the terms of the Treaty of Sèvres signed on Aug. 10, 1920, the League of Nations granted the United Kingdom a provisional *mandate* (order to rule) over Palestine, which would extend west and east of the Jordan River. The British were to help the Jews build a national home and promote the creation of self-governing institutions. The mandate established a Jewish Agency and gave it responsibility for Jewish immigration. In 1922, the League of Nations endorsed the Balfour Declaration and officially approved the terms of the mandate, with the provision that the boundary of Palestine would be limited to the area west of the Jordan River. The area east of the river was made a separate British mandate called Transjordan (now Jordan). The two mandates took effect in 1923.

Under the British mandate, David Ben-Gurion continued to work toward the goal of establishing a Jewish national state in Palestine. Along with fellow Russian-born pioneer Levi Eshkol and others, Ben-Gurion helped create the *Histadrut* (General Federation of Labor) to unite various organizations of farmers, pioneers, and workers. Ben-Gurion served as secretary-general of the Histadrut from 1921 to 1935. Ben-Gurion and Eshkol also supported the creation of the *Haganah*, the secret military force of the Histadrut, in the early 1920's after the British refused to consider establishing an official Jewish armed service.

Ben-Gurion continued to be a voracious reader, spending much of his free time studying Judaism, Christianity, history, politics, and philosophy, and learning such additional foreign languages as Greek and Spanish. He also wrote articles for labor journals and traveled abroad for labor conferences. Ben-Gurion's choices of political and personal activities left him little time to spend with his wife and children, whom he neglected greatly in the early 1920's. Consumed by work, he also resisted helping relatives back in Europe who wanted to relocate to Palestine. In 1925, however, Ben-Gurion's immediate family expanded with the birth of a third child, a daughter named Renana. Also that year, Ben-Gurion's father immigrated to Palestine and settled in Haifa.

The Jewish community in Palestine grew significantly throughout the 1920's and 1930's. It developed a variety of economic, political, and cultural institutions. Ben-Gurion founded the *Mapai* (Israel Workers' Party) in 1930. In 1935, Ben-Gurion became chairman of the Executive of the Jewish Agency. In this position, which he held until

1948, he directed all Jewish affairs in the country. One of his most important challenges involved land development and settlement of immigrants—of whom there were many. More than 100,000 Jewish refugees had come to Palestine from Poland and Germany in the early 1930's to escape the persecution of Jews under the regime of Nazi German dictator Adolf Hitler. This influx alarmed the majority population of Palestinian Arabs, who organized a general uprising against British rule that nearly paralyzed Palestine in the late 1930's.

In 1939, the British imposed strict limitations in Palestine on Jewish immigration and land purchases for the next five years, with any Jewish immigration after that to depend on Arab approval. Jews in Palestine opposed these restrictions, which they believed prevented many Jews in Europe from escaping the increasing persecution there. The situation in Europe worsened on Sept. 1, 1939, when Germany invaded Poland, an action that started World War II (1939–1945). The United Kingdom and France declared war on Germany two days later. Ben-Gurion encouraged young Palestinian Jews to join the British Army fighting with the Allied forces against the Axis powers led by Germany, but he also supported an underground organization that smuggled Jewish refugees into Palestine. During the war, many Palestinian Jews and Arabs joined the Allied forces. In 1940, Ben-Gurion called for the reestablishment of the Jewish Legion, but it was not until 1944 that the British allowed the formation of a Jewish unit of the British Army called the Jewish Brigade.

In May 1942, Zionists from around the world attended a three-day conference at the Biltmore Hotel in New York City. At the conference, Ben-Gurion presented a program he had formulated two years earlier after careful thought and study. Having correctly projected that a new world order would emerge after the war—one in which the United States rather than the United Kingdom would be the most powerful leader of the free world—Ben-Gurion boldly proposed what had never before been officially stated as Zionism's ultimate goal in Palestine—an *independent* Jewish nation. The Biltmore Program, as the adopted resolution became known, also called for unlimited Jewish immigration into Palestine and the development of unpopulated and uncultivated areas, both of which would be carried out under the authority of the Jewish Agency. Differences in interpretation of the Biltmore Program resulted in some conflict between Ben-Gurion and Chaim Weizmann, the president of the World Zionist Organization, which was founded to establish a national homeland in Palestine for the Jewish people. By the fall of 1942, the Jewish community in Palestine found out that the Nazis were implementing a plan of systematic, state-sponsored murder of European Jews as part of their policy called "The Final Solution of the Jewish Question." This horrifying information made the Zionists' struggles for freedom from British rule even more urgent.

The war in Europe ended with the surrender of Germany on May 7, 1945. By that time, the Nazis had killed more than two-thirds of the Jews in Europe—about 6 million Jewish men, women, and children. Among those who survived, many were left homeless and without family. The Zionists wanted the British to allow several hundred thousand of these Jewish survivors to immigrate to Palestine, but the British refused to change the limitations they set in 1939. The Zionists used force to stop the British from blocking the immigration. In 1947, the United Kingdom submitted the issue to the United Nations (UN), an international organization established after World War II to promote world peace.

THE FIRST PRIME MINISTER OF ISRAEL

After considering the situation in Palestine, the UN Special Commission on Palestine made a recommendation that Palestine be divided into an Arab state (including western Galilee, the west bank of the Jordan River, the Gaza Strip, and the Egyptian-Sinai border zone) and a Jewish state (including eastern Galilee, the coastal strip north of Haifa to the Gaza Strip, and the Negev desert). Jerusalem would be placed under international control. The United Kingdom would be expected to end its mandate and leave Palestine no later than Aug. 1, 1948. On Nov. 29, 1947, the UN General Assembly voted to adopt this plan. The Jews in Palestine accepted the UN decision, but the Arabs rejected it. They considered the division a Zionist theft of Arab land. Fighting between Arabs and Jews in Palestine broke out almost immediately.

Ben-Gurion foresaw that war with the Arabs of Palestine and the surrounding countries was inevitable. In mid-1947, while the UN deliberated in preparation for its vote, Ben-Gurion began to make plans for developing the Haganah into a modern regular army and for acquiring aircraft and weapons suitable for warfare. To finance this ambitious military program, an emissary was sent to the United States to raise funds. The chosen emissary was Golda Meir, the acting head of the Political Department of the Jewish Agency. Meir's passionate appeals raised about $50 million (about $454 million today)—nearly twice the amount the agency had hoped for. The Jewish Agency made agreements to buy rifles, machine guns, ammunition, and eventually airplanes, all from Czechoslovakia (now the Czech Republic and Slovakia). Arab attacks on Jewish settlements and supply convoys continued into the spring of 1948. Jerusalem was cut off from the outside world as a result of such attacks. Ben-Gurion marshaled the *Palmach*, the strike force of the Haganah, to drive back the Arabs from their attack positions along the narrow, twisting road leading into Jerusalem, so that Jewish convoys could safely deliver much-needed provisions to the city's people. Ben-Gurion earned great respect as a military leader for his organization of this successful operation. But the fighting went on throughout Palestine.

In the early spring of 1948, in anticipation of the British withdrawal scheduled for May 15, Ben-Gurion established an unofficial provisional government called the People's Administration with himself as its leader. On May 12, the People's Administration convened to decide on the text of the Proclamation of Independence. Ben-Gurion took the lengthy draft presented at the meeting by a committee headed by Moshe Sharett and edited it down to two typewritten pages boldly declaring the existence of a new nation, the State of Israel. The territorial boundaries were not yet known and were not declared. Accompanied by his wife to the Tel Aviv Museum, Ben-Gurion publicly read the official proclamation, broadcast by radio throughout the new state shortly after 4 o'clock in the afternoon on May 14.

Ben-Gurion had little time to savor his new role as prime minister of Israel. On May 15, Arab armies from Egypt, Syria, Lebanon, Transjordan (renamed Jordan in 1949), and Iraq attacked Israel.

Ben-Gurion was not at all surprised. He had been preparing for nearly a year in anticipation of such a reaction to the new nation, and he set about coordinating Israel's defense. By early 1949, Israel had defeated the Arabs and taken control of about half the land the UN had planned for the Palestinian Arab state. Egypt and Jordan held the rest. Egypt occupied the Gaza Strip, a small strip of land on the Mediterranean coast, where Egypt and Israel meet. Jordan occupied the West Bank territory between Israel and the Jordan River. By August 1949, Israel and all five of the attacking Arab states agreed to end the fighting. Although armistice agreements were signed between Israel and Egypt, Syria, Lebanon, and Jordan, there were no formal peace treaties because the Arab nations refused to officially recognize Israel's existence. Israel incorporated the land gained in the fighting into the new country, in the process adding about 150,000 resentful Arabs to its population. About 700,000 Palestinian Arabs became refugees as a result of the conflict. Most of them settled in Jordan, including the West Bank, or in the Gaza Strip. Others went to Syria and Lebanon.

Ben-Gurion (standing) *proclaimed the new Jewish State of Israel in Tel-Aviv in 1948.*

Ben-Gurion served unofficially as prime minister until Israel's first election was held in January 1949 to choose the Knesset, the nation's 120-member parliament. In February 1949, the Knesset elected Chaim Weizmann president. Weizmann then officially appointed Ben-Gurion prime minister. Ben-Gurion also took the position of minister of defense. Under Israel's system of government, the president functions in a largely ceremonial role as head of state. The prime minister is the head of the government and usually the leader of the political party with the most Knesset members. Voters select Knesset candidates by voting for a party list that includes all candidates of a particular party rather than by casting ballots for individual candidates.

As prime minister, Ben-Gurion worked to keep Israel's military strong so that it could resist any future Arab threats. He continued to encourage agricultural settlements like those he experienced earlier in his life, but he also pushed for the development of industry, housing, education, and health services in the cities to support the large flow of Jewish immigrants streaming into the nation. He sought recognition from, and trade with, other nations. Israel joined the United Nations on May 11, 1949

In 1951, Ben-Gurion made the controversial decision to accept war reparations from West Germany. Menachem Begin, leader of the conservative Likud bloc in the Knesset, instigated violent protests in opposition to the decision, which some offended Israelis considered an attempted payoff for the *Holocaust* (the systematic, state-sponsored murder of Jews and others by the Nazis during World War II). Ben-Gurion insisted that the money was compensation only for Jewish property damaged during World War II—money that Israel needed for its continued development. On Jan. 7, 1952, Israel received about $800 million (about $6.1 billion today) from West Germany.

By 1953, the "Old Man," as Ben-Gurion earlier had been nicknamed, was growing weary. He decided that for the sake of his health, he needed to take an extended break from running the government. He believed that the Arabs would not be ready for another large-scale attack on Israel until 1956, so he decided to draw up a detailed defense plan and then take two years off. Ben-Gurion resigned as prime minister in early November 1953 at the age of 67. His party, the Mapai, chose Moshe Sharett to succeed him. Pinhas Lavon became defense minister. In December 1953, David and Paula Ben-Gurion set off for the Negev desert region in southern Israel to take up residence at the Sdeh Boker kibbutz. However, he received regular visits from government and party officials who kept him informed and sought his advice.

In 1953, the "Old Man," as Ben-Gurion was nicknamed, retired to the Sdeh Boker kibbutz in the Negev desert region in southern Israel.

In 1954, a group of Israeli-trained saboteurs were captured by Egyptian security services after trying to firebomb American and British facilities in Alexandria and Cairo in order to disrupt growing amicable relationships between Egypt and the United States and the United Kingdom. The saboteurs hoped that, if Egypt appeared unable to maintain order, the British could be convinced to keep their military presence in the Suez Canal Zone. The Americans had asked the British to withdraw so that the three nations could work cooperatively. The fear of losing the British in the buffer zone posed a consuming threat. The incident took Prime Minister Sharett by surprise because the government had not been consulted before the plan was put into effect. However, the head of Israeli military intelligence, Col. Binyamin Gibli, claimed that the operation was authorized by Defense Minister Lavon, who denied the claim. Sharett appointed a secret inquiry committee to investigate the matter, but the committee could not reach a conclusion regarding the Lavon Affair, as it was later called. Nevertheless, Gibli was transferred to another post, and Lavon was forced to resign his position. As a result of Lavon's resignation, Ben-Gurion was drawn back into the government sooner than expected and reinstated as minister of defense on Feb. 21, 1955. Parliamentary elections were held in July. The Mapai won a majority and chose to make Ben-Gurion prime minister again as well. Sharett became foreign minister. Because of growing concerns amid disagreements over Egyptian military might, Ben-Gurion replaced Sharett with Golda Meir in June 1956.

On July 26, 1956, Egyptian President Gamal Abdel Nasser seized control of the Suez Canal, a narrow, artificial waterway in Egypt that connects the Mediterranean and Red seas and serves as a key shipping route between Europe and Asia. At the time, the canal was owned mainly by the United Kingdom and France. Many nations protested Nasser's action. Ben-Gurion and his closest advisers secretly plotted for several months with representatives of France and the United Kingdom to formulate a plan that would end Egypt's control of the canal. On October 29, Israel invaded Egypt's Sinai Peninsula, which lies between Israel and the Suez Canal, and quickly defeated the

Egyptian forces there. The United Kingdom and France attacked Egypt on October 31. By November 5, the Israelis occupied the Gaza Strip as well as the Sinai Peninsula, and the British and French occupied the northern entrance to the canal. The United Nations called a cease-fire on November 2. The UN ended the fighting, arranged for the foreign troops to withdraw from Egyptian territory, and set up peacekeeping forces in the Sinai and Gaza Strip. Under international pressure, Israeli forces slowly withdrew from the Sinai—ripping up highways, railroad tracks, and telephone poles as they went—and returned the peninsula to Egypt in early 1957. The canal reopened under Egyptian management in the spring of 1957. Israel also withdrew from the Gaza Strip with the understanding, based on an assurance of support from the United States, that UN forces would retain control. But the U.S. ambassador to the UN, Henry Cabot Lodge, did not offer the promised support before the UN General Assembly, and the strip was returned to Egypt. Ben-Gurion was furious.

In 1956, Ben-Gurion authorized the development of nuclear energy in Israel. Although his primary goal was to build nuclear reactors for the production of electric power, he also was aware of the military potential of nuclear energy. In December 1960, the world learned that, with help from France, Israel had built a nuclear reactor in the Negev.

Squabbling within the Mapai and between the Mapai and other parties in the Knesset made governing increasingly difficult for Ben-Gurion in the early 1960's. Meir objected to Ben-Gurion's attempts to bring into the Mapai a group of young men whom she considered overly ambitious, and she argued with him over how to handle relations with Germany. In addition, the Lavon Affair controversy resurfaced in 1960 when new evidence was brought forward to support Lavon's claim that he had not ordered the 1954 acts of sabotage in Egypt. Lavon, who was appointed secretary-general of the Histadrut in 1955, demanded a public exoneration from Ben-Gurion. A committee of seven government ministers was appointed to decide the legal proceedings needed for a matter that happened years ago. Ben-Gurion insisted on a judicial inquiry to settle the issue. When the ministerial committee issued a recommendation to the cabinet in Lavon's favor, Ben-Gurion—still believing that the decision remained in a court of law—did not participate in the voting and requested a leave of absence. Under pressure from the Mapai leadership, Lavon resigned as secretary-general of the Histadrut. The embittered Ben-Gurion resigned as prime minister on June 16, 1963, despite appeals to remain in power from his political allies and from such top army officers as General Yitzhak Rabin. Finance minister Levi Eshkol succeeded him.

After his resignation from the government in 1963, David Ben-Gurion retired to the Sdeh Boker kibbutz. But he remained a member of the Mapai and continued to follow his country's political developments from the desert. On June 29, 1965, at a meeting of his supporters held at Sdeh Boker, Ben-Gurion broke away from the Mapai and declared the establishment of a new political party called the *Rafi* (Israeli Workers' List). Most of his supporters, including key aides Shimon Peres and Moshe Dayan, affiliated themselves with the Rafi, but Ben-Gurion and his Rafi associates won only 10 Knesset seats in the next election.

Full-scale war erupted between Israel and its Arab neighbors in 1967, but Ben-Gurion played no role in planning or executing the successful Israeli strategy that quickly won the war. In the late 1960's, his health began to decline. He also was saddened by the death of his wife on Jan. 29, 1968. Ben-Gurion remained a member of the Knesset until 1970, when he resigned and retired at the kibbutz.

Ben-Gurion spent his final years reflecting and writing about his life and his country. His book *Memoirs* (1970) was transcribed from a series of personal interviews recorded at Sdeh Boker. He wrote *Israel: A Personal History*, published in 1971. Later that year, Prime Minister Golda Meir led the nation in a celebration of Ben-Gurion's 85th birthday. Ben-Gurion published *My Talks with Arab Leaders* in 1972. He died on Dec. 1, 1973, about two weeks after suffering a stroke. In accordance with his wishes, his funeral was marked by silence. He was buried at Sdeh Boker next to his wife, in the land of Israel he helped create. ■

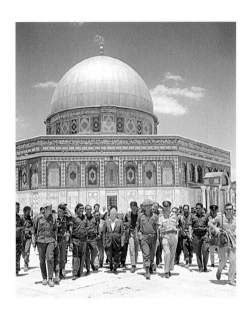

On June 7, 1967, Ben-Gurion, shown center in gray suit and hat, *and Yitzhak Rabin led a group of soldiers past the Dome of the Rock on the Temple Mount in Jerusalem, on a victory tour following the Six-Day War fought against Egypt, Jordan, and Syria.*

Chronology of Meir's life

1898	born May 3 in Kiev, Ukraine
1906	moves to Milwaukee with family
1913	runs away from home to live with sister's family in Denver, Colorado
1917	moves to Chicago to help energize Poalei Zion Jewish workers movement there; marries Morris Meyerson in Milwaukee
1921	goes to Palestine to join a kibbutz
1924	son Menachem born in Jerusalem
1926	daughter Sarah born in Jerusalem
1929	elected a delegate to the Zionist Congress
1930	joins Mapai (Israel Workers' Party) and assumes key role in new party
1934	joins Histadrut Executive (executive body of the Histadrut)
1948	the new nation of Israel is established in a part of Palestine; appointed minister to the Soviet Union by Israeli Foreign Minister Moshe Sharett
1949	becomes Israel's minister of labor; Israel joins United Nations
1956	becomes Israel's minister of foreign affairs; changes married last name Meyerson to Hebraized Meir
1966	becomes secretary-general of Mapai
1968	helps form Israel Labor Party and becomes party leader
1969	becomes prime minister of Israel
1973	leads Labor Party to victory in December elections in Israel
1974	resigns as prime minister in June
1975	autobiography *My Life* published
1977	attends premiere of biographical Broadway play *Golda*, about Meir's life, in November
1978	dies December 8 in Jerusalem of lymphatic cancer

Golda Meir (1898–1978)

Golda Meir *(may EER)* was one of the most important leaders of Israel. She became prime minister in 1969 at the age of 70, after a long career of service to the nation she dreamed of as a child and helped bring into reality in 1948.

Born with the last name of Mabovitz, she took her husband Morris's last name of Meyerson after they married in 1917. She adopted the last name Meir, a Hebraized (made into Hebrew) version of Meyerson, in 1956. But throughout her life, what people called her most often was simply Golda.

Meir exuded a charismatic presence through both her appearance and her speaking ability. Meir spoke in a straightforward manner, usually without a prepared text. This spontaneous style gave her delivery a heartfelt quality that helped her establish an emotional connection with listeners and persuade them to adopt her point of view.

As the first female prime minister of Israel, and one of few women in the world to hold a nation's highest political office, Meir was a trailblazer for the women's movements of the 1960's and 1970's. She also served as a strong female role model simply by the way she lived, particularly while she was a member of an egalitarian farming community as a young woman. Throughout her life, Meir believed herself to be equal to any man and proved it many times over.

Israel occupies a narrow strip of land in southwestern Asia on the eastern shore of the Mediterraean Sea. Israel was founded in 1948 as a homeland for Jews from all parts of the world. Israel makes up most of the Biblical Holy Land, the place where the religious and national identity of the Jews developed. Jerusalem is Israel's capital and largest city.

Chapter 1: Goldie in the Goldena Medina

Golda Meir was born Golda Mabovitz on May 3, 1898, in Kiev, Ukraine. At this time, Ukraine was controlled by Russia. Golda's father, Moshe Yitzhak Mabovitz, had been educated at a *yeshiva* (Jewish rabbinical seminary) and was a skilled carpenter. Her mother, Bluma Neiditz Mabovitz, gave birth to eight children, but only three survived beyond infancy, all of them girls: Shana, Golda, and Tzipka. Shana was nine years older than Golda, and Tzipka was four years younger. Golda was named after a strong-willed great-grandmother who died shortly before Golda was born. In her early life, Golda was called "Goldie." She inherited her mother's beauty and her great-grandmother's strong will. Goldie grew up speaking Yiddish, the German-dialect, Hebrew character language used by nearly 90 percent of the Jews in Europe during the late 1800's and early 1900's.

Kiev is an attractive, historic city nestled on the hilly western bank of the Dnieper River. But in the late 1800's and early 1900's, much of that appeal was lost on the city's Jews, who were a persecuted ethnic minority. Beginning in 1881, many Jews in Russia were killed in a series of organized massacres called *pogroms (poh GROMZ or POH gruhmz)*. In her autobiography, *My Life* (1975), Meir recalled her intense fear of pogroms as a child.

> *I must have been very young, maybe only three and a half or four. We lived then on the first floor of a small house in Kiev, and I can still recall distinctly hearing about a pogrom that was to descend on us. I didn't know then, of course, what a pogrom was, but I knew it had something to do with being Jewish and with the rabble that used to surge through the town, brandishing knives and huge sticks, screaming "Christ killers" as they looked for the Jews, and who were now going to do terrible things to me and my family.*

> *I can remember how I stood on the stairs that led to the second floor, where another Jewish family lived, holding hands with their little daughter and watching our fathers trying to barricade the entrance with boards of wood. That pogrom never materialized, but*

to this day I remember how scared I was and how angry that all my father could do to protect me was to nail a few planks together while we waited for the hooligans to come. And, above all, I remember being aware that this was happening to me because I was Jewish, which made me different from most of the other children in the yard. It was a feeling that I was to know again many times during my life—the fear, the frustration, the consciousness of being different and the profound instinctive belief that if one wanted to survive, one had to take effective action about it personally.[1]

Another vivid memory from Meir's early childhood was of hunger. As a result of the pervasive *anti-Semitism* (prejudice against Jews) in Russia, Goldie's father had a hard time finding work, and thus the family often had little money with which to buy food. They ate mostly potatoes and bread, and there was rarely enough to satisfy the hunger.

By 1903, Moshe Mabovitz was tired of the poverty and persecution in Kiev. He decided that he would go to the *goldena medina*—that is, the "golden land"—of America, where he had heard that even for Jews, work and food were plentiful. There he thought he could make a fortune in just a few years, and then return to his family with enough money for them all to live comfortably. In 1903, he sold his furniture and tools to buy the cheapest available ticket, in steerage class, on a ship bound for the United States. It was a long, uncomfortable trip, traveling below deck in a dark, stuffy cargo hold packed with nearly 2,000 other poor passengers. The ship docked at Ellis Island in New York Harbor, and Mabovitz entered the United States through the immigration station there. With help from the Hebrew Immigrant Aid Society, he eventually settled in Milwaukee, Wisconsin, where he found work as a carpenter with the railroad. He regularly sent money back to his family in Russia.

When Moshe left for the United States, Bluma and the girls moved to Pinsk, Bluma's hometown in Russia (now part of Belarus). They lived at first with Bluma's parents, who ran a tavern where Goldie finally got enough to eat. Goldie especially enjoyed the Friday night Sabbath dinners, when numerous aunts, uncles, and cousins joined in the family meal. Bluma made money by selling homemade bread and cakes door to door, and eventually she was able to afford lodging for herself and her daughters in a house near the police station. Pinsk was located in the *Pale of Settlement,* a crowded area along Russia's western border where Jews were ordered to live. The city had muddy, unpaved streets, but it bustled with mercantile activity. From time to time, elite cavalry warriors called *Cossacks* who served in the Russian army rode their horses through the streets of Pinsk, brandishing their swords and shouting anti-Semitic remarks at the Jews. One day they came thundering down the street where Goldie and some friends were playing. The Cossacks' horses did not stop but instead leaped over the heads of the crouching, terrified children.

In Pinsk, little Goldie looked up to her teen-age sister Shana, who taught her to read, write, and do basic arithmetic. Shana soon became involved in the revolutionary movement that had been sweeping across Russia since the 1890's, when a series of bad harvests caused starvation among rural peasants. Lack of food and the country's increasing industrialization led to a growing discontent among the rising middle class and workers in the cities. Shana believed that the overthrow of the Russian *czar* (emperor) and the replacement of czarist rule with a socialist form of government (in which the government controls or owns the major means of production and distribution) would lead to improved living conditions for the common people. Shana also became a follower of *Zionism,* a movement to establish a Jewish national state in Palestine, the ancient Jewish homeland, where the Jews lived from as early as 1800 B.C. until about A.D. 135, when they were driven out by the Romans. *Zion* is the poetic name for Palestine in Hebrew, the biblical language of the Jewish people. Many Jews favored Zionism as a means of escaping anti-Semitism. Shana joined a group of young revolutionaries who held secret meetings to discuss socialist and Zionist ideas. Shana held these meetings at her house while her mother was away at the *synagogue* (Jewish temple). Goldie would hide from her sister and eavesdrop on the meetings. Although she did not understand everything

A young Goldie Mabovitz is shown in her earliest known portrait taken in Pinsk, 1904.

they said, their revolutionary zeal made a lasting impression on her. But she also knew how dangerous these secret activities could be, because the family could hear at the nearby police station the screams of those who were beaten after they were caught.

Bluma decided that instead of waiting for Moshe to return, she and the girls should flee the turmoil of Russia and join him in Milwaukee. After much preparation, they set off on the long journey to the United States in the spring of 1906. Moshe could not afford official Russian government exit permits for them, but he was able to secure faked passports and pay their passage to the United States. Bluma, Shana, Goldie, and Tzipka departed Pinsk by train. Bluma had to bribe the Russian guards at Galicia at the Russian-Polish border before the four of them were allowed to cross into Poland. The train continued through Poland and Austria-Hungary into Belgium, where they boarded a ship at the port city of Antwerp. They made the 14-day ocean crossing in a dark, stuffy, below-deck cabin shared with four other people—not luxurious accommodations, but better than the steerage passage Moshe had endured three years earlier. They were allowed to go up on deck, and Goldie stood there watching the sea for hours. She was the only member of her family who did not get seasick during the voyage. The ship docked at Quebec, Canada, and they took a train from there to Milwaukee.

YOUTH AND EDUCATION

Soon after their arrival in Milwaukee in 1906, the Mabovitz family moved into a two-room apartment at 615 Walnut Street in the city's Jewish section. The apartment had no electricity, but it did have running water, which was a step up from Pinsk. Eight-year-old Goldie was amazed by many of the things Americans took for granted that she had never seen before, such as ice cream, soda pop, brightly colored clothing from a department store, and a five-story "skyscraper." When Moshe first picked up his wife and daughters at the train station, he drove them home in an automobile. It was Goldie's first car ride. Bluma and the girls knew almost no English when they arrived in Milwaukee, but many of the people in the neighborhood also spoke Yiddish, which eased the family's transition into American life. Moshe, who had Americanized his name to Morris, continued his carpentry work for the railroad. Bluma opened and ran a small grocery store at 623 Walnut Street. Shana got a job making buttonholes by hand at a tailor shop. When Bluma went to the market early in the morning to buy her grocery supplies, Goldie was left to mind the store, standing on a box behind the counter to wait on customers. She hated working at the store in the morning because it made her late for school. Eventually the local truant officer convinced Bluma that it was against the law for her to prevent her daughter from getting to school on time. Bluma then got up earlier to complete her trips to the market before school started, and Goldie became much happier. At the Fourth Street School she attended through eighth grade, she quickly learned to speak English and easily made friends with other students. She also studied German, a required subject in the Milwaukee public schools because people of German descent made up a large portion of the city's population. Her other courses included reading, spelling, arithmetic, and music.

Shana was not as successful as her younger sister was in their new land. As she entered her late teens, Shana wanted to continue her education. However, her parents thought that higher education for girls was not important and instead wanted her to help out at home and work in the grocery store. Shana defiantly left home and took a series of clothing factory jobs. But the sweatshop conditions under which she worked caused her health to deteriorate, and she eventually contracted tuberculosis. At that time, this infectious bacterial disease, also called *consumption,* had no cure and was treated with fresh air, rest, mild exercise, and healthy food, all of which she received in Denver, Colorado, at the National Jewish Hospital for Consumptives. Shana's boyfriend from Pinsk, Shamai Korngold, was able to join her in Denver, and they married after she recovered. The couple later had a baby daughter. Although Shana and her parents were not on speaking terms at the time, she exchanged letters with Goldie through Goldie's close friend Regina Hamburger.

In 1908, at the age of 11 and in the fourth grade, Goldie was already destined for a career in politics when, she recalled in her autobiography: "I got involved in my first 'public work.' Although school in Milwaukee was free, a nominal sum was charged for text-books, which many of the children in my class could not afford. Obviously, someone had to do something to solve the problem, so I decided to launch a fund. It was to be my very first experience as a fund raiser, but hardly the last!"[2] Goldie organized a group of girls from the school, who called themselves the American Young Sisters Society, and persuaded the owner of the local Packen Hall to let them hold a public meeting there. The girls painted posters and delivered invitations to the meeting. Dozens of people came, and Goldie's first public speech was a great success. The crowd donated money to help buy books, and the group's efforts were even written up in a Milwaukee newspaper. Goldie enclosed a clipping with a letter to Shana. In the spring of 1912, Goldie was valedictorian of her grade school graduating class at the Fourth Street School. Over the summer, Goldie and her friend Regina worked full-time at a department store in downtown Milwaukee. They also taught English to Polish and Romanian Jewish immigrants for 10 cents an hour. Goldie had become a fluent speaker of English, and her voice had little trace of a foreign accent.

Goldie was ready for high school in the fall of 1912. She wanted to earn her diploma and then become a teacher. But she encountered the same resistance from her parents that Shana had faced earlier. Her mother in particular thought high school was a waste of time for a girl. Furthermore, at that time, Wisconsin state law forbid female teachers to continue teaching after they married. Because it was assumed that Goldie should marry—the sooner the better, as far as Bluma was concerned—then becoming a teacher would be a waste of time, too. Bluma suggested that Goldie attend a secretarial school and then work in an office as a typist until she got married. Bluma even set about to matchmaking, choosing a real estate agent about twice Goldie's age as a prospective husband for her daughter. Goldie despaired at her mother's attitude but resolved not to let it stop her from pursuing her dreams. Against her parents' wishes, she enrolled at North Division High School and began her classes for the fall semester. But the arguments with her parents persisted. She expressed her frustration over this course of events in letters to Shana and Shamai. A letter from Shamai dated November 15 marked a turning point in Goldie's life. In it, Shamai urged Goldie to come out to Denver, where he and Shana would do all they could to help her pursue her education and career plans. Shana seconded the invitation. Goldie knew her parents would never consent to it, but she wanted to go, so she decided to run away from home.

For several months, Goldie carefully plotted her escape. Shana sent her some money, but it was not enough for the train ticket Goldie needed. She taught some more English lessons and borrowed from an older friend to make up the difference. Goldie's friend Regina became her accomplice in the scheme. At bedtime on the eve of Goldie's departure, Goldie lowered a small suitcase packed with clothes out her bedroom window to Regina, who took it, boarded a trolley to the train station, and hid the suitcase in the baggage department. The next morning, Goldie left for school, took the trolley to Union Station, where she retrieved the hidden suitcase, and boarded the train to Denver. She left behind a note for her parents telling them where she had gone and not to worry. Goldie took heart from the words in the last letter she received from Shana before departing for Denver: "Always be calm and act coolly. This way of action will always bring you good results. Be brave."[3] She heeded this advice at the time and in the years to come.

Goldie arrived in Denver in February 1913. She enrolled at North Side High School, where she earned A's in English, Latin, German, algebra, ancient history, and music. Although Goldie lived with Shana, Shamai, and their 2-year-old daughter, Judith, in their apartment in the Jewish community on the west side of Denver, most of the students at the high school were not Jews. But Goldie had little time to get involved with mainstream American teen-agers from school. As soon as her classes were over every school day, she went straight to work at Shamai's dry-cleaning business while he went off to a second, part-time job as a janitor. Later in the evenings, Shana and Shamai often entertained a group of Russian Jewish immigrants at their apartment. They carried on lively discussions in Yiddish about philosophy and politics.

Although much of the conversation went over Goldie's head, she listened intently when the topic shifted to socialism. She was interested in the ideas of the American socialist and labor movement activist Eugene Debs, who at that time had run unsuccessfully for president of the United States four times as the candidate of the Socialist Party. But even more interesting to her were the stories about Zionist pioneers, especially those who established *kibbutzim* in Palestine. Kibbutzim are Jewish communities based on the idea of social and economic equality. Members of each kibbutz share ownership of all the kibbutz's means of income production, including businesses and land. The first kibbutz was founded in 1909 in the Jordan River Valley, south of the Sea of Galilee, by Jewish immigrants from Europe. Goldie admired the way these Zionist pioneers set about building the national Jewish state with their own hands.

Goldie's presence did not go unnoticed by the young men in the evening discussion group, most of whom were single. She looked older than her age—she turned 15 in the spring of 1913—with her womanly figure, bluish-gray eyes, firm jaw, and long, reddish-brown hair. Many of the young men asked her out on dates. The one who most piqued her interest was 20-year-old Morris Meyerson, a quiet, gentle fellow who wore wire-rim glasses and had a seemingly boundless knowledge of literature and music. He had immigrated from Lithuania with his family as a boy, and in Denver he eked out a living as a sign painter to support himself, his widowed mother, and three sisters, one of whom had been Shana's roommate at the hospital. Shana approved of Morris as her sister's boyfriend, but she thought Goldie was beginning to spend too much time on her social life and not enough time on her studies. However, the energetic Goldie was maintaining good grades and thought Shana was getting much too bossy about her personal life. Finally, after a clash in the spring of 1914, Goldie angrily walked out of the apartment and did not come back.

With nothing but the clothes she was wearing, 16-year-old Goldie was suddenly on her own. She accepted an invitation to live in the cramped apartment of a couple she knew who were suffering from the last stages of tuberculosis. Amazingly, she did not contract the highly communicable disease. To live independently, however, Goldie realized she would have to stop attending high school and find a full-time job. She worked at first stretching out lace curtains in a laundry and then found a better job in a department store taking measurements for custom-made skirt linings. That job enabled her to move out of her friends' apartment and rent a small room of her own. Goldie and Shana broke several months of silence and resumed speaking to each other. Goldie and Morris spent a lot of time together reading at the library, attending lectures, enjoying free concerts in city parks, and taking long walks, hand in hand.

In the spring of 1915, Goldie was surprised to receive a letter from her father. She had had little contact with her parents since leaving Milwaukee. Meir described the letter in her autobiography: "It was very short and to the point: If I valued my mother's life, he wrote, I should come back home."[4] After talking the matter over with Morris, Goldie decided to go back to Milwaukee. He would try to join her later after his sister, who was still in the hospital, recovered from her tuberculosis. Meir recalled: "One night, before I left, Morris told me shyly that he was in love with me and wanted to marry me. I explained happily and just as shyly that I loved him, too, but that I was still much too young for marriage, and we agreed that we would have to wait. In the meantime, we would keep our relationship a secret and write to each other all the time."[5]

After Goldie returned to Milwaukee, her parents no longer objected to her pursuit of higher education. She reenrolled at North Division High School, happily rejoining her friend Regina. Goldie helped her father raise money for the People's Relief Committee as World War I (1914–1918) raged across Europe. Her parents had become involved in local Zionist activities and often entertained speakers from the movement in their home. After spotting Goldie at a lecture one day, a young Zionist approached her about joining the Jewish workers' movement *Poalei Zion* (Workers for Zion). She was not ready for such a commitment at that point, but she agreed to teach Yiddish language and culture to children at the Poalei Zion Folkschule, a Yiddish school. By the summer of 1915, at the age of 17, she had joined Poalei Zion. Although Morris had known when

Goldie Mabovitz, shown far right, stands with members of the Poalei Zion Folkschule in Milwaukee in 1916.

YIDDISCH FOLKS SCHULE
MILWAUKEE WIS. JULY 16

they were together in Denver of Goldie's interest in Zionism, he did not share her enthusiasm for it and told her so in a letter. He thought the idea of a Jewish homeland in Palestine was an unrealistic dream. But Goldie was not deterred.

Goldie graduated from high school in 1916, and then enrolled at the Milwaukee Normal School (now University of Wisconsin-Milwaukee) for a career in teaching. She also continued her activism in Poalei Zion. She argued with her father over her plans to stand on a soapbox at a street corner and make a public speech promoting Zionism. Despite her assurances that soapbox speeches were a common and acceptable form of political discourse in the United States, he threatened to pull her down off the box by her hair braid and drag her home. Goldie gave the speech anyway. Her father did show up, but he was so impressed with her eloquent and persuasive speaking ability that he forgot about dragging her away. Meir later reflected, "I consider that to have been the most successful speech I ever made."[6]

Finally, Morris moved to Milwaukee. He and Goldie each rented a room on the same street and resumed dating. They went to the park, the beach, the opera, and other cultural attractions, much as they had in Denver, but in Milwaukee there were also Zionist lectures and meetings, some of which Morris grudgingly attended with Goldie. Their tastes conflicted one Saturday night, when Goldie was eager to attend a speech by the visiting Poalei Zion activist David Ben-Gurion, who had been a pioneer in Palestine and was touring the United States to persuade others to immigrate. Goldie also was scheduled to host a luncheon for Ben-Gurion the next day. But Morris long before had bought tickets for himself and Goldie to attend a Saturday night performance by the visiting Chicago Symphony Orchestra. Feeling she had a duty to honor her promise to attend the concert, she skipped the speech. The next morning, the Zionist leaders informed her that the luncheon had been canceled. Meir later recalled: "It wasn't proper, they said, that a person who couldn't be bothered to hear Ben-Gurion speak—and of course, I was too embarrassed to explain the extremely personal reason for my absence—should have the privilege of entertaining him for lunch. I was heartbroken but thought that they were perfectly right, and I accepted their verdict stoically."[7]

By 1917, Goldie had made up her mind that she wanted be a Zionist activist in Palestine. She dropped out of the teachers school, got a job at a local library, and devoted even more time to Poalei Zion activities. Goldie knew that it would take several years to save up the money for her passage to Palestine, but she also knew that unless Morris agreed to go with her, there would be no point in marrying him. She begged him to go with her, but he wanted more time to think about it before making such a commitment. Soon afterward, two Poalei Zion leaders, Ben Shapiro and Baruch Zuckerman, asked Goldie to move to Chicago to help energize the movement there. She agreed and parted ways with Morris.

MARRIAGE AND ZIONISM

In Chicago, Goldie lived with the Shapiro family in an apartment at 1306 Lawndale Road, a block away from busy Roosevelt Road in the heart of the Jewish community. There she was reunited with her sister Shana, who had relocated from Denver with her family in

1916. Goldie's friend Regina also moved to Chicago. Goldie's work for Poalei Zion often lasted from the evening into the wee hours of the following morning. To allow herself time to sleep late in the morning, she got an afternoon job at the local branch of the Chicago Public Library. Goldie was happy to be among so many people she liked, doing work she enjoyed, yet she missed Morris. He missed her, too, and soon he moved to Chicago to be near her. Events in Palestine soon changed his mind about the feasibility of Zionism as well.

Although the Jews were among the earliest peoples to inhabit Palestine, other groups laid claim to the area throughout its history. After the Romans drove the Jews out of Jerusalem in A.D. 135, most of the Jews in the rest of Palestine fled, except for small communities in the northernmost region of Galilee. In the A.D. 300's, the Byzantine Empire took control of the region. Its rulers were Christian. Over time, Christianity spread to most of Palestine. In the 600's, Muslim Arab armies from the south conquered most of the Middle East, including Palestine. Until the early 1900's, Palestine was controlled by a series of Muslim powers, the last of which was the Ottoman Empire. In World War I, the Ottoman Empire fought on the side of Germany and Austria-Hungary against the Allies led by France, the United Kingdom, and Russia. As the war continued, the British hoped to take control of Palestine because of its location near the Suez Canal, which links the Mediterranean Sea and the Red Sea. In an effort to gain support from Jewish leaders in the United Kingdom, the United States, and other countries, British Foreign Secretary Arthur James Balfour issued a government document called the Balfour Declaration on Nov. 2, 1917. It read as follows:

His Majesty's Government view with favour the establishment in Palestine of a national home for the Jewish people, and will use their best endeavors to facilitate the achievement of this object, it being clearly understood that nothing shall be done which may prejudice the civil and religious rights of existing non-Jewish communities in Palestine, or the rights and political status enjoyed by Jews in any other country.

Zionists were overjoyed. With the British backing their claim, they thought, the Jewish homeland would soon become a reality. Morris at last told Goldie that he would go to Palestine with her when the time came. Then he asked her to marry him, and she said yes. They were wed on Dec. 24, 1917, by a rabbi in a traditional Jewish marriage ceremony, standing under a *huppa,* a canopy that symbolizes the union of the bride and groom. In keeping with the couple's desire for a simple ceremony, the wedding took place at the home of Goldie's parents with only a few family members and close friends in attendance. Goldie was 19 years old, and Morris was 24. Goldie changed her name from Golda Mabovitz to Golda Meyerson. Golda and Morris moved into an apartment at 1311 Chestnut in Milwaukee.

Being married made no difference in Golda's work for Poalei Zion. She resumed her active schedule, often traveling out of town to speak on behalf of the movement. In 1918, Golda served as a delegate from Milwaukee to the first American Jewish Congress in Philadelphia. By 1918, the British had captured Palestine from the Ottoman Empire. After World War I ended, anti-Semitism in Ukraine (which was still under Russian control) and Poland resulted in an outbreak of pogroms there. Golda heard that 40 Jews in Pinsk had been lined up against a wall and shot during one of the pogroms. Outraged, she organized a public protest march against the pogroms. On March 22, 1919, thousands of Jews representing 50 organizations marched together in downtown Milwaukee, followed by a band and a color guard of army veterans bearing American and Zionist flags. Many non-Jews also participated in the march, and the crowd watching the parade seemed supportive. Protest marches had not yet become a common form of public demonstration in the United States, so the event garnered national attention.

Golda Mabovitz and Morris Meyerson were married in 1917. Although they separated in 1938, they never divorced. The couple is shown in a 1918 photo taken in Chicago, where Golda had moved in 1916.

In January 1920, the League of Nations was established. It was an international association of countries created to maintain peace among the world's nations. Under the terms of the Treaty of Sèvres signed on Aug. 10, 1920, the League of Nations gave the United Kingdom a provisional *mandate* (order to rule) over Palestine. Under the mandate, the British were to help the Jews build a national home and promote the creation of self-governing institutions. The mandate included the establishment of a Jewish Agency and gave it responsibility for Jewish immigration. The Jewish community of Palestine under the British mandate was called the *yishuv*.

In September 1920, the Meyersons moved to New York City in anticipation of their immigration to Palestine. They shared an apartment in the Morningside Heights neighborhood with Golda's friend Regina and her husband, Yossel Kopelov, who was also a friend of Morris. All four of them found jobs to raise the remaining money needed for their passage: Golda as a librarian, Morris as a sign painter, Regina as a secretary, and Yossel as a barber. All the while, Golda maintained her activism in Poalei Zion. By the spring of 1921, they were ready to depart. Golda and Morris made the rounds to say good-bye to family and friends—first to Philadelphia, where Morris's mother and sisters had moved from Denver; then to Milwaukee, home of Golda's parents and many of their friends; and finally to Chicago, where Golda's sister Shana and her family lived. By then, Shana and her husband Shamai had a son, 3-year-old Chaim, in addition to their daughter, Judith, who was 10. Shamai noticed how attentively Shana listened to Golda's detailed description of her plans. He jokingly asked his wife if she would like to go to Palestine, too, and to everyone's surprise, she replied that she would. Although Shana's behavior as an adult became more conservative after she took on the responsibility of parenthood, she had retained the Zionist roots of her youth. Shana proposed that she and the children accompany Golda and Morris while Shamai would stay behind to keep working. He would send them money until they were settled, at which point he would join them. Realizing it was useless to argue, Shamai agreed. Golda was overjoyed. They returned to New York and prepared to set sail.

Chapter 2: Immigration to Palestine

On May 23, 1921, Golda and Morris Meyerson boarded the S.S. *Pocahontas* in New York City to begin their journey to Palestine. Traveling with them were Golda's sister Shana Korngold with her two children and the couple's friends Regina and Yossel Kopelov. Getting there proved to be quite an adventure. The ship's first stop was Boston, but it took about a week to get there, mainly because the mutinous crew sabotaged the engines in protest that their concerns about the vessel's unseaworthiness were being ignored. The ship remained docked in Boston for more than a week for repairs, during which time the captain fired most of the engineers and some of the crew. He probably should have replaced all of them, because sabotage to the ship's pumps, boilers, and refrigerators—spoiling much of the food—continued as the *Pocahontas* made its way across the Atlantic Ocean. Golda tried to keep everyone's spirits up by leading the passengers in singing folk songs. A fellow passenger taught her some folk songs in Hebrew. On June 16, the ship limped into port at Ponta Delgada on São Miguel Island in the Azores (a group of islands in the North Atlantic that belong to Portugal), for another round of repairs. As the passengers disembarked, four crew members were overheard bragging about their plans to sink the ship when the voyage resumed, and the captain shackled them in irons. Ponta Delgada seemed like paradise after the hellish conditions aboard the ship. The passengers were greeted by a group of bearded, Portuguese-speaking Sephardic Jews who lived on the island. *Sephardic* Jews—that is, descendants of Jews from Spain, Portugal, or other Mediterranean countries and the Middle East—make up one of two broad groups of Jews. Golda and her party belonged to the other group, the *Ashkenazic* Jews—that is, descendants of members of Jewish communities of central and Eastern Europe. They used hand gestures to get around the language barrier, and the Sephardic Jews graciously showed their guests around the island. The travelers were thrilled to find fresh fruit and fish and clean water. Golda and Morris took walks together and enjoyed the beautiful scenery. But about a week later, it was time to reboard the repaired ship. Rough seas and further equipment failures hampered the rest of the voyage. By the time the *Pocahontas* arrived at its final destination of Naples, Italy, on July 5, the captain was dead—reportedly a victim of suicide, though some passengers suspected murder.

Golda and her shipmates had made it across the ocean at last, but the group of 19 prospective pioneers heading for Palestine had more traveling ahead of them. They stayed for five days in Naples, enjoying such cultural attractions as the San Carlo Opera House and stocking up on supplies they would need in Palestine, including mosquito netting and oil lamps. In Naples, they discovered that their baggage was missing, including the large trunks that carried most of their possessions. Travel officials promised they would locate the baggage and send it on the next ship, and the group went on without it. The group took a train across Italy from Naples to the port city of Brindisi, on the coast of the Adriatic Sea, to catch a ship bound for Alexandria, Egypt. The trip passed swiftly and without incident. In the historic city of Alexandria, which was occupied by the British at the time, Golda saw *mosques* (buildings used for Muslim worship) and camels for the first time. In her autobiography, Meir also recalled: "On the way to the station we got our first taste of the Middle East at its worst: crowds of beggars—men, women, and children wrapped in filthy rags and covered with flies. They made me think of the beggars who had so terrified me in Pinsk, and I knew if one of them actually touched me, I would scream—pioneer or not."[1] But somehow she and her group made it onto the train for the hot, dusty overnight trip, the final leg of their long journey. They arrived in Tel Aviv in the scorching midday heat on July 14, nearly two months after leaving New York.

Standing at the train station away from the heart of town, surrounded by a desolate expanse of sand, with the sun blazing down on them, the newcomers suddenly felt at a loss. Now that they were finally here, they did not know what to do. The friends from Tel Aviv who were supposed to meet them at the station were not there. Golda's 10-year-old niece, Judith, began to cry, perhaps expressing how all of them felt at that moment. Then a man came up and, speaking in Yiddish, introduced himself. He owned a small, modest hotel nearby where they could stay. As the bedraggled group walked to the hotel, Golda saw a lone tree poking up out of the sand and was heartened by the thought that if that tree could survive here, so could they.

KIBBUTZ LIFE

Golda had expected to join a kibbutz—specifically, Kibbutz Merhavia, where Golda and Morris knew one member who had emigrated from the United States—within a week or two of her group's arrival. But when she contacted the kibbutz, she was told to wait until the end of the summer to apply for membership. In the interim, Golda and Shana found a two-room apartment in Tel Aviv for the seven of them. They borrowed bedding and pots and pans. Shana stayed home to cook, keep house, and look after the children. The others got jobs: Golda teaching English lessons, Regina as a secretary, Yossel as a barber, and Morris as a bookkeeper at a British public works installation in Lydda, where he stayed during the week and then came home on weekends. Their lost luggage from Naples arrived in September, containing Morris's precious phonograph and records. Some of the neighbors, who at first had found these American newcomers strange for covering their windows with screens to keep out the ubiquitous flies, began to drop by to drink tea and listen to music with them. After their rough start, they began to feel more at home.

In Tel Aviv, Golda finally met David Ben-Gurion. She was part of a small group that eagerly gathered at his second-floor room one afternoon to hear his report on his recent trip to Russia. By then, Ben-Gurion was a prominent Zionist leader in Palestine and secretary-general of the *Histadrut* (General Federation of Labor), which he had helped create.

In the fall of 1921, the 32 men and 8 women of Kibbutz Merhavia voted against admitting Golda and Morris, doubting whether the Americans would be able or willing to handle the strenuous labor of their collective farm village. But Golda persisted, and the members finally decided to allow them in for a trial period before a final decision would be rendered. Shana was not keen on the communal lifestyle of the kibbutzim and opted to keep her household in Tel Aviv. Yossel did not want to join a kibbutz, and Regina's initial interest in the idea waned after she discovered that being a skilled secretary fluent in English paid very well. Yossel and Regina decided to remain in Tel Aviv. The Meyersons were on their own at the kibbutz.

Kibbutz Merhavia was an agricultural settlement in the highlands of Galilee—the northernmost part of Palestine—in a mountain valley beyond Mount Tabor, near Nazareth. After a hot, dry summer, the parched landscape of the kibbutz looked rather bleak when the Meyersons arrived. A cement fence with openings for guns surrounded the settlement, providing protection against occasional attacks from Arab villagers in the region. As a married couple, Golda and Morris had a room of their own, but the unmarried members of the kibbutz shared communal quarters. Everyone ate together in a common dining room, washed in a communal shower, and dressed in clean clothes taken from shelves in one central location. Children were raised as a group in their own communal quarters, where they slept, played, and studied. Adults rotated jobs in the fields, in the kitchens, in the laundry, and on guard duty, with no differentiation of tasks between men and women. The first objective of Kibbutz Merhavia was to clear the rocks from the soil and drain the mosquito-ridden swamp in order to establish a collective farm from which the kibbutz would derive its income.

The Meyersons passed their trial period and were voted into the kibbutz as full-fledged members. Golda plunged in with gusto at Kibbutz Merhavia. In the fields, she picked and shelled almonds, planted saplings, and tended chickens, all without complaining, even though the work left her exhausted at the end of the day and she hated chickens. She convinced the others that breeding their own chickens and selling their own eggs instead of buying them from Arab traders would be profitable for the kibbutz, and it was. While other women of the kibbutz disdained kitchen work as demeaning, Golda accepted the task enthusiastically and took steps to improve the quality of the food, which she considered

Golda Meyerson is shown working in the fields of the Kibbutz Merhavia in Palestine in 1921.

"frightful."[2]   For example, she eliminated the bitter olive oil they had been using and, at breakfast, she replaced canned herring with hot oatmeal. After a visit to Shana in Tel Aviv, she brought back a bag of oranges for a rare treat. Others snickered when she insisted on draping the table with a sheet and adding a centerpiece of fresh wildflowers for the weekly Sabbath meal, but no one complained about the cookies she added on Friday nights. Gregarious Golda easily adapted to the social and political life of the kibbutz. In 1922, she was elected to the Histadrut and chosen to represent Merhavia at a weeklong convention of kibbutzim. There she reencountered Ben-Gurion and met many other leaders of the Jewish labor movement. Her dedication and enthusiasm won her admiration despite her colossal gaffe of speaking Yiddish instead of Hebrew—the language advocated by Zionists for the new Jewish state—in addressing the convention. Because of her fluency in English, however, Golda was sometimes called upon to serve as translator and guide for British dignitaries visiting Palestine. In 1922, the League of Nations endorsed the Balfour Declaration and declared that the boundary of the British mandate of Palestine would be limited to the area west of the Jordan River. The area east of the river, called Transjordan (now Jordan), was made a separate British mandate. Both mandates took effect in 1923.

While Golda flourished at Kibbutz Merhavia, however, mild-mannered Morris did not. The other members did not share his interests in music, literature, and philosophy, and the lack of privacy bothered him greatly. He and Golda had little time to themselves. Although both Morris and Golda wanted to have children, Morris did not want them raised by a committee and refused to start a family while they were living at the kibbutz. Golda considered this refusal a betrayal of his initial agreement to live on a kibbutz, because communal child rearing was a known part of that lifestyle. This conflict strained their marriage. But the worst problem was Morris's inability to keep up with the strenuous physical demands of kibbutz labor. He frequently fell ill and, in 1923, he suffered an attack of malaria so serious that it landed him in a hospital in Tiberias, on the shore of the Sea of Galilee. As Golda worried at his bedside, doctors there ordered that he give up manual labor. That meant leaving the kibbutz. In her autobiography, Meir reflected:

> It was a great wrench for me to leave the kibbutz, but I consoled myself tearfully by hoping that we would both be back soon, that Morris would regain his health quickly, that we would have a baby and that the relationship between us—which had so deteriorated in Merhavia—would improve. If all this happened, I told myself, then leaving the kibbutz for a while was a very small price to pay. Unfortunately, it did not work out that way.[3]

TEL AVIV AND JERUSALEM

The Meyersons left Kibbutz Merhavia in 1923 and moved to Tel Aviv. While Morris recuperated from his illness, Golda got a part-time job as a cashier in the Solel Boneh construction company (originally known as the Office of Public Works and Construction). Neither of them wanted to end their marriage, yet they both were miserable in it. Morris had gone to Kibbutz Merhavia because of Golda, and it nearly killed him. Golda had left Kibbutz Merhavia because of Morris, and she missed it terribly. But they preferred to suffer in irritable silence rather than attempt to openly discuss their differences. David Remez, head of the Solel Boneh, had met Golda briefly at the kibbutz convention, and he helped secure a bookkeeping job for Morris in the company's Jerusalem office. Golda stayed in Tel Aviv because they needed the money from both jobs, and Morris came back on weekends. Morris urged Golda to get a job in Jerusalem and join him there. Finally Remez found a job for Golda with the Solel Boneh in Jerusalem as well. Just before she left Tel Aviv, she found out she was pregnant. Menachem Meyerson was born on Nov. 23, 1924, in Jerusalem. Golda and Morris were happy to become parents, and the arrival of the baby improved their marriage—for a few months. But Golda's Zionist interests still preoccupied her. In the spring of 1925, she gave in to her yearnings and returned to Kibbutz Merhavia, taking the baby, whom she breast-fed, with her. Morris did not try to stop her but remained in Jerusalem. However, kibbutz life was different for Golda the second time around. Instead of working the land, she was assigned to take care of the babies—her own and four others—which deprived her of adult company much of the time. It also was not the same without Morris, and she felt unsettled without him.

In her autobiography, Meir describes reaching a critical turning point:

> To put it very bluntly, I had to decide which came first: my duty to my husband, my home and my child or the kind of life I myself really wanted. Not for the first time—and certainly not for the last—I realized that in a conflict between my duty and my innermost desires, it was my duty that had the prior claim. There was really no other alternative than to stop pining for a way of life that couldn't be mine, so I returned to Jerusalem . . . determined to make a fresh start.[4]

Despite Golda's good intentions, life in Jerusalem was miserable for the Meyerson family. They lived in a grubby two-room apartment with no gas or electricity in a run-down Arab neighborhood. One of the rooms they sublet to a boarder because they needed the money. The kitchen was in a tin shack outside. An oil stove was used for cooking and heat, a kerosene lamp for light. Water was drawn from a well and had to be boiled before drinking. The Solel Boneh got into financial trouble and started paying Morris mainly in credit slips, which the landlord would not take and other businesses would accept only at less than face value. After Golda became pregnant for the second time, the family's financial situation worsened. Golda quit her job, and they stopped renting to their boarder so that they could use the second room themselves. Golda and Morris's daughter, Sarah Meyerson, was born in May 1926. When Menachem was old enough for preschool, Golda could not pay his tuition but bartered his way in by doing the laundry of all the school's children. Still in need of money, she got a job teaching English at a private school. While Menachem was in school, she brought Sarah with her to work because she could not afford a baby sitter. Shana and Shamai, who had joined his family in Tel Aviv, brought cheese and fresh fruit and vegetables whenever they visited.

By 1928, the stress of four years of poverty had further eroded Golda and Morris's crumbling marriage. Golda felt disconnected from the Zionist movement that had brought her to Palestine in the first place, and she was disappointed that Morris had not developed an interest in it as she had hoped. But Morris had hoped that Golda would lose what he considered her obsessive interest in the movement once they had a family, and then they could all return to the United States and enjoy a better life. With such conflicting wishes, their marriage was doomed. Then Golda received a job offer as secretary to the Moetzet Hapoalot (Women's Labor Council) of the Histadrut in Tel Aviv. She took it.

Morris stayed in Jerusalem and visited his family on weekends. Golda and Morris would not separate until 1938, and they never divorced (Morris died in 1951). But when they parted ways in 1928, they knew that their love for each other alone was not enough to save their marriage.

Chapter 3: Zionist Leadership

Golda Meyerson and her two children moved into a small apartment in Tel Aviv in 1928 after she accepted the job as secretary of the Moetzet Hapoalot, or Women's Labor Council. This job would be the first of many steps in her climb toward the top leadership position of her country. Although she continued to use the last name of Meyerson until 1956, her accomplishments in public life are most commonly cited under the name of Meir.

Meir served as secretary of the Women's Labor Council from 1928 to 1932. The council established agricultural training farms for young immigrant women who came to work the land in Palestine but had no experience in farming. In addition to their vocational training, the women received instruction in Hebrew and support in adjusting to the way of life in Palestine. Meir traveled throughout Palestine to set up the training farms, and she also took trips to the United States to coordinate the Women's Labor Council activities with those of its American sister organization, the Pioneer Women.

STRIKING A BALANCE

Meir's children, Menachem and Sarah, attended a school run by the labor movement. Meir hired a baby sitter to care for the children after school until she got home from work, which sometimes was long after they went to bed. Meir took the children to concerts and movies whenever she could. The children looked forward to the weekend visits from their father, who spent much of his time with them reading them books and talking about music. Meir's sister Shana, who also lived in Tel Aviv, often looked after Menachem and Sarah when Meir took longer trips. Meir's parents, who had immigrated to Palestine from the United States in 1926, also visited from time to time. Meir loved her children, but she also loved her Zionist work. Striking a balance between home and work responsibilities was challenging at times.

She described the challenges for the working mother in an article she wrote anonymously for a collection of memoirs called *The Ploughwoman* (1930):

> *In spite of the place which her children and her family take up in her life, her nature and being demand something more; she cannot divorce herself from a larger social life. . . . And for such a woman, there is no rest. . . . But the mother suffers in the very work she has taken up. Always she has the feeling that her work is not as productive as that of a man or even of an unmarried woman. The children, too, always demand her, in health and even more in sickness. And this eternal inner division, this double pull, this alternating feeling of unfulfilled duty—today toward her family, the next day toward her work—this is the burden of the working mother.*[1]

Meir was elected a delegate to the Zionist Congress in 1929 and to most of the congresses after that. The Zionist Congress is the supreme governing body of the World Zionist Organization (WZO), the official organization of the Zionist movement. Founded by the Zionist leader Theodor Herzl in 1897, the WZO functioned somewhat like a government for the Jewish community of Palestine during the British mandate and worked to establish a national homeland for the Jews. Chaim Weizmann presided over the World Zionist Congress that Meir attended in 1929. Subsequent congresses during her lifetime were convened in 1931, 1933, 1935, 1937, 1939, 1946, 1951, 1956, 1960, 1965, 1968, 1972, and 1978.

In 1930, Meir joined the *Mapai* (Israel Workers' Party) and soon assumed a key role in the new party. The Mapai was founded by David Ben-Gurion from the merger of two smaller political parties, Ahdut Haavoda and Hapoel Hatzair. During the British mandate, the Mapai combined Zionist and socialist ideas in promoting the establishment of a Jewish national state. At that time, the Mapai was the driving force behind the labor movement, including the *Histadrut* (General Federation of Labor). Meir, a skilled and persuasive fund-raiser, made many trips to Europe and the United States during the 1930's to solicit money for the Zionist movement on behalf of the Mapai and the Histadrut.

In 1932, Meir accepted a two-year assignment to work with the

Pioneer Women, helping the organization add new chapters throughout the United States to give it a national scope. But what really brought her to the United States was an attempt to save her daughter's life. Sarah had been diagnosed by doctors in Palestine as suffering from a kidney disease for which they had no cure. Meir and her husband together decided that Meir should seek medical treatment for Sarah at an American hospital before giving up all hope. Although the two-week ocean crossing was dangerous for Sarah, her parents thought it was worth the risk. Despite Sarah's condition, the children enjoyed having their mother all to themselves for a change, and the trip went smoothly. The doctors at Beth Israel Hospital in New York City confirmed that Sarah indeed had a kidney disease, but it was not the fatal one the doctors in Palestine thought she had. Sarah was cured within six weeks. Meir and her children lived in two of the five boroughs into which New York City is divided: the first year with friends in Brooklyn and the second year with friends in Manhattan. Meir enrolled the children in school. Because he knew no English, 8-year-old Menachem initially was placed in the same first-grade class as his 6-year-old sister. For their first week at school, their mother sat in the classroom with them and translated the teacher's words into Hebrew to ease the children's transition. They learned English quickly. Meir took them to the zoo and to many museums and other cultural attractions in New York City. But her work for the Pioneer Women often kept her out of town for weeks at a time. The Great Depression, a worldwide economic slump of the 1930's, made fund-raising difficult. However, Meir's own experiences with poverty and hunger contributed to a simple sincerity in her speeches that moved people to give whatever they could spare. Meir made many friends among the Pioneer Women. One of them with whom she had become especially close, Leah Biskin, went with her when she and her children returned to Palestine in 1934. Meir's husband resumed his regular weekend visits and was delighted when Menachem began to take lessons to learn how to play the cello. The pretense of the marriage was abandoned in 1938, and Morris no longer visited the children; the children now visited their father in Haifa, to where he had relocated from Jerusalem after getting a new job.

Meir joined the Histadrut Executive, the governing executive body of the Histadrut, in 1934. Soon afterward, the Executive elected her to the Central Committee, the Histadrut's cabinet. Meir had reached the inner circle of Histadrut leadership. Mapai founder Ben-Gurion, who had headed the Histadrut as secretary-general since 1921, left the post in 1935 to become chairman of the Executive of the Jewish Agency. His successor as secretary-general of the Histadrut was David Remez, with whom Meir had developed a close personal relationship over the years since they had worked together at the Solel Boneh in the early 1920's. Meir thus both directly and indirectly wielded considerable influence in the Histadrut. She chaired the branch of the Histadrut that was responsible for providing medical service, and she also helped the Histadrut address the issues of working conditions and unemployment problems among Jewish laborers. As both a labor union body and a major employer, the Histadrut played an important role in developing the economy of the Jewish community in Palestine.

ALIYAHS AND WORLD WAR

Jewish immigration became a serious issue in Palestine in the 1930's. This issue had been building toward a crisis for more than 50 years. Under the Ottoman Empire, the population of Jews in Palestine had reached about 24,000 by 1880. In 1882, in response to the pogroms in Russia, groups of Jewish youths calling themselves *Hoveve-Zion* (Lovers of Zion) started a movement to promote emigration from Europe to Palestine. Early Jewish immigrants from the Zionist movement came to Palestine in waves. Each wave of immigrants was called an *aliyah*, a word meaning *ascent* or *going up*, derived from Judaism's idea of *assumption*—that is, a religious belief that a certain person was taken bodily into heaven. About 25,000 Jews, most of them Zionists from Eastern Europe, arrived in the First Aliyah from 1882 through 1903, doubling Palestine's Jewish population. About 35,000 more, including Ben-Gurion and other Zionists, came in the Second Aliyah from 1904 through 1918. In 1914, at the beginning of World War I, Palestine's total population of 700,000 consisted of about 85,000 Jews and 615,000 Arabs, most of whom were Muslims. The Arabs initially paid little attention to the Jewish immigrants other than to trade with them. Inland from the coastal plain, Palestine at that time was sparsely populated, and many of the Jewish settlements were established in less-populated areas. However, as Jewish settlements continued to spring up throughout the land, the Arabs began to feel that the Jews were encroaching too greatly on their territory. This resentment of the Jews' presence led to Arab attacks on many of the kibbutzim and other settlements. About the time that the Balfour Declaration was issued in 1917, the British promised independence to various Arab groups in the Middle East. The promises were vague, but Arab leaders assumed they included Palestine. In the meantime, Jewish immigration continued. Another 35,000 Jews, including Meir and many of her family members and friends, arrived in the Third Aliyah from 1919 through 1923. By the end of this aliyah, the British mandates of Palestine and Transjordan were in effect. However, the terms of the Palestine mandate were not clear, and various parties interpreted it differently. The disagreements continued through the rest of the 1920's and into the 1930's. Many Zionists believed that the British were not doing enough to promote a Jewish national home, especially when the British imposed some restrictions on Jewish immigration and land purchases. However, the leaders of a growing Arab nationalist movement claimed that the Balfour Declaration allowed for a Jewish homeland only if the Arabs agreed to it, and the Arabs opposed the idea of a Jewish national home. The Arabs rejected British proposals for self-governing institutions in Palestine, and so none were created. In the early 1930's, political conditions in Europe worsened for Jews, particularly after the anti-Semitic National Socialist, or Nazi, Party of Adolf Hitler came to power in Germany in 1933. To escape the Nazi persecution, more than 100,000 Jewish refugees flooded into Palestine from Germany and Poland during the early 1930's. This sudden huge influx alarmed the Palestinian Arabs. Their attacks against Jewish settlements intensified, and they organized a general uprising against British rule during the late 1930's that nearly paralyzed Palestine.

During an Arab strike in 1936, the British closed Palestine's main port at Jaffa. Remez and Meir came up with the idea of the

Histadrut opening a port in nearby Tel Aviv. But to build the docks, train the dockworkers and sailors, and establish a fleet of ships, they would need money. Meir spent much of 1937 on a successful fund-raising tour in the United States.

By the late 1930's, the British found themselves in an untenable position on the issue of Jewish immigration in Palestine. On the one hand, the Jews continued to press for a Jewish national homeland and protested British restrictions on Jewish immigration. On the other hand, the Arabs remained staunchly opposed to any sort of Jewish state in Palestine and rioted against the British for allowing in so many Jews. The Arabs still made up the majority of Palestine's population and were violent in their protests, so the British decided to appease them in an effort to stop the riots. On May 17, 1939, the British government published a brief policy statement known as a "white paper" (so called because it was submitted to the British House of Commons without the traditional blue cover used for longer documents) in which it announced it would drastically limit Jewish immigration to 75,000 Jews for the next five years. Any Jewish immigration after that would depend on Arab approval. The House of Commons approved the white paper on May 23. At the 21st Zionist Congress that Meir attended in Geneva, Switzerland, from August 16 to 25, Jewish leaders condemned the white paper. On September 1, Germany invaded Poland, an action that set off World War II (1939–1945). Two days later, the United Kingdom and France declared war on Germany. With the onset of war, the plight of Jews living in and around Germany became even more perilous. But the British would not change the immigration policy outlined in the white paper. Nevertheless, Ben-Gurion declared: "We will fight with the British against Hitler as if there were no White Paper; we will fight the White Paper as if there were no war."[2]

Meir followed Ben-Gurion's approach. In her autobiography, she recalled viewing the challenge ahead as being made up of three struggles:

> There was the desperate struggle to get as many Jews as possible into Palestine, the humiliating battle we were forced to fight in order

to persuade the British to let us take part in military action against the Nazis, and finally the struggle—in the face of almost total British indifference—to preserve the yishuv's economy so that we could somehow emerge from the war strong enough and healthy enough to be able to absorb a large immigration—provided there were any Jews left to immigrate.[3]

As head of the Histadrut's political department, Meir negotiated with the British for better wages and working conditions on behalf of the Jewish and Arab workers who belonged to the Histadrut. With her Histadrut background, her fluency in English, and her skill in human relations, Meir soon became the chief spokesperson for the Jewish community in dealing with the British in many matters. But she also engaged in organized secret efforts to smuggle in as many Jews from Europe as possible, provide them with forged identification papers, and disperse them throughout Palestine. Like many other teen-agers in the yishuv, Meir's daughter, Sarah, joined the Youth Movement, which engaged in its own clandestine efforts to defy the British restrictions, such as putting up posters on behalf of the *Haganah,* the secret military force of the Histadrut. Sarah later dropped out of high school to join a kibbutz. By the fall of 1942, horrifying news had reached the Jewish community in Palestine about the Nazi implementation of a policy labeled "The Final Solution of the Jewish Question." This policy called for the elimination of every Jew—man, woman, and child—under German rule, using a systematic, state-sponsored plan of mass murder. The Jewish community in Palestine intensified its struggle for freedom from the British, who still refused to budge from the immigration limits set by the 1939 white paper.

Meir, already prominent among the leadership of the Jewish community, became more widely known to the public after testifying in a September 1943 court trial. The defendants were two young Jews accused of stealing British army weapons for the Haganah. Meir refused to be bullied by the British prosecutor's grilling, insisting that the Jewish community was "interested in this war and in the victory of the British forces"[4] and considered stealing from the army a crime, while providing firm but evasive responses to questions for which direct answers could have been incriminating. In general terms, she upheld the Jews' right to self-defense. Meir did not let the judge, called president of the court, intimidate her, either. In the English-language newspaper *The Palestine Post* (which later became *The Jerusalem Post*) dated Sept. 7, 1943, the lengthy account of the trial included the following interchange:

> **Major B. [Baxter, the prosecutor]:** *Did Haganah also have arms before the outbreak of the war?*
>
> **G. M. [Golda Meir]:** *I do not know, but I suppose so. There were also riots before the war.*
>
> **President [of the Court]:** *I ask you to limit yourself only to what concerns this case and not to go backwards, or otherwise we'll soon be back two thousand years ago.*
>
> **G. M.:** *If the Jewish question had been solved two thousand years ago . . .*
>
> **President:** *Keep quiet!*
>
> **G. M.:** *I object to being addressed in that manner.*
>
> **President:** *You should know how to conduct yourself in court.*
>
> **G. M.:** *I beg your pardon if I interrupted you, but you should not address me in that manner.*[5]

When Meir visited her parents the next day, her mother said that her father had been out in the neighborhood all morning showing off the newspaper and bragging about "my Golda." Before long, others were referring to her the same way.

PARTITIONED PALESTINE

World War II ended in Europe with the surrender of Germany on May 7, 1945. By then, the Nazis had killed about 6 million Jews—more than two-thirds of the Jewish population of Europe. Many of those who managed to survive were left without homes or family. Meir was among the Zionist leaders who begged the British to allow several hundred thousand of these Jewish survivors to immigrate to Palestine, but the British stood by the white paper limits. The Zionists began to use force to stop the British from blocking the immigration of war refugees. There were three main Jewish resistance groups: the Haganah; the

Irgun Zvai Leumi (National Military Organization), which was known for engaging in violent guerrilla tactics; and the Lohamei Herut Yisrael (Fighters for the Freedom of Israel), also known as Lehi or the Stern Gang, which was led by Avraham Stern, to engage in aggressive acts against the British. British authorities dealt harshly with any resistance members they caught.

On Oct. 24, 1945, the United Nations (UN) was established as an organization of nations that works for world peace and security and the betterment of humanity. On March 25, 1946, Meir testified before a UN commission consisting of British and American representatives sent to Jerusalem to conduct hearings regarding Jewish immigration to Palestine. The commission had already interviewed Jews who were living in camps for displaced persons in Europe to verify their desire to immigrate to Palestine. Now they wanted to gauge the willingness of Palestine's Jewish community to receive them. Noting that Meir was the only woman to testify before the committee, *The Palestine Post* reported that she "dispelled the uncomfortable court-room atmosphere, the irritation and the boredom that had latterly prevailed. The Committee and audience listened with keen attention to the witness who represented the Histadrut."[6] Meir began by stating, "I am authorized on behalf of the close to one hundred and sixty thousand members of the Histadrut to state here in the clearest terms that there is nothing that Jewish labor is not prepared to do in this country in order to receive large masses of Jewish immigrants, with no limitations and with no conditions whatsoever."[7] She went on:

> *I don't know, gentlemen, whether you who have the good fortune to belong to the two great democratic nations, the British and the American, can, even with the best of will to understand our problems, realize what it means to be the member of a people whose very right to exist is constantly being questioned. . . . We want only that which is given naturally to all peoples of the world, to be masters of our own fate—only of our fate, not of the destiny of others; . . . to have the chance to bring the surviving Jewish children, of whom not so many are left in the world now, to this country so that they may grow up like our youngsters who were born here, free of fear, with*

heads high. Our children here don't understand why the very exist-ence of the Jewish people as such is questioned. For them, it is natu-ral to be a Jew.[8]

In April 1946, the British pressured Italian authorities to bar the departure of two Haganah ships bearing more than 1,000 Jewish refugees bound for Palestine from the coast of Italy. The refugees declared a hunger strike and refused to leave their ships, vowing to kill themselves and sink the ships if they were not allowed to enter Palestine. Meir proposed that Palestine's Jewish community show its solidarity with the refugees by having the leaders of its main organizations fast as well. Her proposal passed. She and 12 other leaders—10 men and 2 women—set up cots at the Jewish Agency headquarters in Jerusalem and refused all food except for one ball of matzoh the size of an olive to fulfill the religious requirements of the ceremonial *seder* meal for Passover, which fell on the third day of the fast. The protesters drank unsweetened tea twice a day to avoid dehydration. They also allowed themselves cigarettes, for which Meir, who by then was a smoker, was grateful. Their fast attracted worldwide media attention. Shortly after their 100th hour of fasting had passed, they received word that the refugees would be allowed to enter. The ships left the Italian coast under heavy British guard on

Jewish immigrants, arriving in Haifa aboard a refugee ship in early 1948, wave the flag of the future State of Israel.

May 8. Later that month, the UN commission published its report, recommending that 100,000 Jewish immigrants be allowed to enter Palestine immediately. The U.S. government agreed with the recommendation. But British Foreign Minister Ernest Bevin, fearing a renewed outbreak of Arab rioting, refused to abide by it. At a Histadrut conference soon afterward, Meir condemned the British rejection of the commission's decision. "In that case, we shall have to prove to Mr. Bevin that unless his policy is altered, he will have to send an army division to fight *us.*"[9] To underscore the Jews' defiance, a Haganah operation at midnight on June 16 simultaneously blew up all the bridges on the frontiers of the mandated territory, effectively severing the land links between Palestine and the outside world and temporarily isolating the British administrators there.

On Saturday, June 29, 1946—a date that became known as "Black Saturday" in the Jewish community—British forces launched Operation Broadside. Its goal was to round up and arrest Jewish leaders throughout Palestine and seize any weapons or incriminating documents that could be found. With 100,000 troops supported by tanks and armored cars, British forces raided homes in the cities and attacked kibbutzim in the countryside. By the end of the day, nearly 3,000 leaders had been arrested, many of them beaten in the process. Jewish Agency head Ben-Gurion was not one of them—he happened to be in Paris that day at a conference—and, much to her surprise, neither was Meir. But Moshe Sharett, the head of the Jewish Agency's Political Department, and as such second to Ben-Gurion in the agency's chain of authority, was among the leaders imprisoned in the heavily fortified detention camp at Latrun, near Jerusalem. Meir was selected to take Sharett's position. She promptly announced the desire of the Jewish community for freedom from British rule. Then she met with the British high commissioner to open negotiations for the release of the imprisoned Jewish leaders. Meir maintained contact with Ben-Gurion, who remained in Paris to avoid arrest in Palestine, and smuggled messages into and out of the detention camp with the help of a milkman. She secretly stayed in touch with resistance leaders outside the camp as well. Concerned that the more militant Irgun and Lehi resistance forces would resort to terrorism—a strategy she categorically opposed—she came up with a plan of widespread civil disobedience similar to the campaign of nonviolent resistance being used successfully by the great Indian leader Mohandas Gandhi against British rule in India. But she could not convince other key Jewish leaders to endorse this plan. Instead, they backed a proposal by Irgun leader Menachem Begin to humiliate the British by blowing up a key government building, the King David Hotel, on July 22 after giving everyone in the building half an hour to evacuate. But no one heeded Begin's repeated telephone warnings to leave the building that day, and the explosives planted in the hotel basement went off while hundreds of people were still inside, killing 91 and wounding many more. The furious British became even more resolute in their refusal to cooperate with the Jews. On August 12, they announced that any illegal immigrants apprehended in the waters surrounding Palestine would be deported to Cyprus or some-where else—even, as in the tragic case of the 4,500 refugees aboard the ship *Exodus* the following year, back to Germany. But Jewish refugees from Europe continued to flock to Palestine, even at the risk of beatings or deportation. At the 22nd Zionist Congress held Dec. 9–24, 1946, Meir praised the refugees for their courage. She urged the World Zionist Organization "to demand that full measure of political independence which can only be attained through the estab-lishment of a Jewish state."[10]

On Feb. 14, 1947, the British government submitted its problems with the Jews and Arabs in Palestine to the United Nations. The UN Special Commission on Palestine that was formed to study the situ-ation submitted its report on August 31. It recommended that Palestine be *partitioned* (divided) into an Arab state and a Jewish state, with Jerusalem placed under international control. The United Kingdom would be expected to end its mandate and leave Palestine no later than Aug. 1, 1948. Meir, who moved to Jerusalem in September 1947, was unhappy with the idea of a Jewish state with-out that city as a part of it, but she reluctantly supported the parti-tion plan in the hope that once it was in place, the Jews and the Arabs might be able to live in peace. On Nov. 29, 1947, as Meir lis-tened to the proceedings on the radio, the UN General Assembly voted to adopt the commission's recommendation. Zionist leaders in Palestine accepted the UN decision. But Arab governments and the Palestinian Arabs rejected it. They considered the partition a theft of Arab land by the Zionists and the governments that supported them. Fighting broke out almost immediately.

Ben-Gurion, who had returned to Palestine by 1947, foresaw even before the UN decision that war between the new Jewish state and the Arabs of Palestine and the surrounding countries was inevitable. In mid-1947, he started making plans to develop the Haganah into a modern regular army and to acquire weapons and aircraft suitable for warfare. Once again the Jewish Agency would look to the United States for financing. The Jewish Agency Executive, the governing body under Ben-Gurion, elected Meir to approach the leaders of the American Jewish community, once more calling upon her fluency in English and her ability to make speeches that resonated with her audiences. The Jewish Agency treasurer, Eleizer Kaplan, told the Executive to expect no more than about $7 million (about $64 million today) from the fund-raising campaign, although Ben-Gurion hoped for $25 million to $30 million (about $227 million to $272 million today). Meir brought back $50 million (about $454 million today), an accomplishment Ben-Gurion later credited as critical to the early survival of the new nation. Another aspect of the Jewish Agency's early planning was an attempt to secretly negotiate with King Abdullah I of Transjordan (now Jordan) in the hope of securing from him a promise to refrain from joining the other Arab nations in attacking the new Jewish state once it came into existence. With 18,000 British-trained, well-armed soldiers and 400 tanks, Transjordan's Arab Legion was the strongest military force among the Arab nations at that time. Transjordan also had a frontier force of 15,000 men under British command. In early November 1947, Meir met with the king at a private home near the Jordan River, where Abdullah assured Meir that his country would not join the attack. They agreed to meet again after the UN resolution passed. However, after the partition was approved, Abdullah decided that he would join the other Arab states in opposing the new Jewish state. Meir made a second, highly secret attempt to dissuade him. Disguised as an Arab peasant woman, she journeyed to Transjordan's capital of Amman to meet with the king on May 10, 1948. Abdullah expressed polite regret that he could not back out of his alliance with the other Arab nations. Meir said: "If Your Majesty has turned his back on our original understanding and wants war instead, there will be war. Despite our handicaps I believe that we will win. We will meet again after the war, and after there is a Jewish state."[11] Four days later, there was a Jewish state.

Chapter 4: Serving the New Nation

The British mandate of Palestine was set to expire on May 15, 1948. In anticipation of the British departure, the general council of the World Zionist Organization established a provisional government for the new Jewish state in April. This government's legislature—known as the People's Council, National Council, or Provisional State Council—had 37 members, including Meir (as Golda Meyerson), its only female member. The executive branch, called the People's Administration or National Administration, had 13 members and was headed by Jewish Agency Executive chairman David Ben-Gurion. In her autobiography, Meir described the assessment of the situation offered by Jewish military leaders from the Haganah at a meeting of the People's Council on May 12: "We could be sure of only two things: The British would pull out, and the Arabs would invade."[1] The Haganah chief of operations, Yigael Yadin, put the Jews' chances of surviving the Arab onslaught at "fifty-fifty."[2] Meir recalled:

> So it was on that bright note that the final decision was made. On Friday, May 14, 1948 (the fifth of Iyar, 5078, according to the Hebrew calendar), the Jewish state would come into being, its population numbering 650,000, its chance of surviving its birth depending on whether the yishuv could possibly meet the assault of five regular Arab armies actively aided by Palestine's 1,000,000 Arabs.[3]

Meir started the day on May 14 in Tel Aviv with a meeting of the People's Council in which the group discussed the name of the new nation and the final wording of the document that would declare its independence. She returned to her seaside hotel at about 2 o'clock in the afternoon. She washed her hair, put on her best black dress, and spent a few moments in quiet contemplation before heading over to the heavily guarded Tel Aviv Museum, where the official proclamation was to be read and signed. The place and time of the ceremony were officially kept secret from all but the group of about 200 carefully selected individuals who were invited, but word of the historic event had leaked out, and a crowd of thousands had gathered in the area in anticipation. The ceremony began at 4:00 p.m. sharp. Ben-Gurion, dressed more formally than usual in dark suit and tie, stood up at the head of the T-shaped table and rapped his gavel. Everyone stood and sang "Hatikva" ("The Hope"), the traditional Jewish song that would become the national anthem. Then he began the reading of the 979-word proclamation in Hebrew, which took about 15 minutes and was broadcast by radio throughout the land. The proclamation included a statement that the new nation would be open to the immigration of Jews throughout the world, which drew thunderous applause, and an appeal to the Arabs of the region for peace and mutual cooperation. It declared, "Accordingly we, members of the People's Council . . . do hereby declare the establishment of a Jewish state in Evetz-Israel [Land of Israel], the State of Israel."[4]

In the awed silence that followed, an elderly rabbi suddenly rose and recited the traditional Hebrew prayer of thanksgiving. Applause and cheers erupted both inside and outside the building. Meir recalled her thoughts at that moment:

Golda Meyerson signs the proclamation establishing the State of Israel on May 14, 1948, in Tel Aviv.

> *The State of Israel! My eyes filled with tears, and my hands shook. We had done it. We had brought the Jewish state into existence—and I, Golda Mabovitch Meyerson, had lived to see the day. Whatever happened now, whatever price any of us would have to pay for it, we had re-created the Jewish national home. The long exile was over. . . . It seemed to me that no Jew on earth had ever been more privileged than I was that Friday afternoon.[5]*

The signers of the proclamation were called up in alphabetical order by last name. Tears streaming down her face at the thought of "all those who should have been here today and are not,"[6] Meir added her name—still Golda Meyerson at that time—to the document. Only two women were among the 25 people who signed the proclamation that day: Meir and Rachel Cohen, who chaired the Women's International Zionist Organization. That evening, while many Israelis sang and danced in the streets, Meir and some friends quietly toasted the new nation with a glass of wine at the hotel. Meir knew that when the mandate expired at midnight, the British would leave the new State of Israel to fend for itself against the Arab armies that were sure to attack within hours. Shortly after midnight, Meir was heartened by a phone call with the news that U.S. President Harry S. Truman had recognized the State of Israel. Recognition from the Soviet Union, of which Russia became a part in 1922, followed soon afterward.

As dawn was breaking at about 5:00 a.m. on May 15, 1948, Meir saw four Egyptian planes racing across the sky. Noise of bombs exploding followed. Israel was under attack by Arab armies from Egypt, Syria, Lebanon, Transjordan (renamed Jordan in 1949), and Iraq. Israel fought back. The next day, Meir received a telegram from Henry Montor, the vice president of the United Jewish Appeal in the United States and a man with whom she had developed a close personal relationship during her fund-raising trip earlier that year. He urged her to come back and speak to the American Jews who were eager to support Israel's war effort. Ben-Gurion, who had become prime minister of Israel, agreed that additional U.S. funds would be vital, and so Meir left on the next available flight to New York. Toward the end of her successful mission about a month later, a car collided with the cab in which Meir was riding to Brooklyn. Her leg was fractured in the accident, and she spent several weeks with it in a cast at the New York Hospital for Joint Diseases.

GOVERNMENT MINISTER

In June 1948, Israeli Foreign Minister Moshe Sharett appointed Meir minister to the Soviet Union. She returned to Israel from the United States during a UN-sponsored cease-fire that lasted from mid-June to mid-July. In Tel Aviv she assembled her staff. To her pleasant surprise, the Israeli government appointed her daughter, Sarah, as a radio operator on her staff. Sarah's boyfriend from the kibbutz, Zechariah Rehabi, a fellow radio operator and a specialist in code, also was appointed. Before the delegation left for Moscow, the couple married in a simple ceremony at the home of Meir's sister Shana Korngold. Also in attendance were Meir's son, Menachem, who was soon to serve in the newly formed Israel Defense Forces; her estranged husband, Morris Meyerson; and her elderly mother, Bluma Mabovitz.

In June 1948, Israeli Foreign Minister Moshe Sharett appointed Meir minister to the Soviet Union. She was Israel's first ambassador to the Soviet Union. Sharett is shown greeting Meir after her appointment.

Meir and her staff arrived in Moscow in September 1948. Meir was nervous about her assignment. Her Russian was rusty, and she had no training in the formalities of international diplomacy, but she forged ahead. She ran her staff quarters like a kibbutz. Many nations had yet to officially recognize Israel, and Meir did her best to form cordial relationships with diplomats from other countries as well as with the Soviets. She also tried to establish contact with the Jews living in Moscow. Although the practice of religion was strongly discouraged under the Soviet Union's Communist system of government, Jews on the street furtively murmured words of support, and about 50,000 Soviet Jews turned out for the Rosh-Hashanah services Meir attended at the synagogue in Moscow. The ecstatic throng inside the synagogue and on the street in front reached out to her. The Soviet government was not pleased. In January 1949, it closed down the Yiddish theater and suspended Yiddish publications. The Moscow Jews then kept their distance from the Israelis.

Back in Israel, the new nation held its first election in January 1949 to select the Knesset, the country's 120-member, one-house parliament. Under Israel's system of government, voters select a party list that includes all candidates of a particular party rather than casting ballots for individual candidates. Seats in the Knesset are then allocated proportionally according to the percentage of the vote received by each list. The leader of the party with the most Knesset seats usually becomes prime minister. In Israel, the prime minister is the head of Israel's government. The country also has a president, elected by the Knesset, who functions in a largely ceremonial role as head of state. In February 1949, the Knesset elected Chaim Weizmann president. He then officially appointed Ben-Gurion prime minister. Ben-Gurion's Mapai party had won the most Knesset seats in January. Even though Meir was in Moscow at the time, her name had been included on the Mapai list, so she won a seat in the Knesset—a seat she would retain for 25 years. As Ben-Gurion formed his cabinet in February, he offered Meir the post of minister of labor. She accepted. She briefly returned to Israel to take the oath of office on March 11, 1949, with the other government officials and then went back to Moscow to wrap up her affairs there. She made her final departure from Moscow on April 20, 1949. Israel joined the United Nations on May 11, 1949.

By the time Meir returned to Israel to assume her new post, Israel had defeated the Arabs and gained control of about half of the land that the 1947 UN partition plan had designated for the Palestinian Arab state. Egypt and Jordan occupied the rest of Palestine. Egypt controlled the Gaza Strip, a small piece of land along the coast of the Mediterranean Sea, where Egypt and Israel meet. Jordan held the West Bank, a territory along the Jordan River between Israel and Jordan. In Jerusalem, Israel controlled the western half of the city and Jordan the eastern half. By August 1949, all five of the Arab states that had attacked Israel had agreed to stop the fighting, and Israel had signed armistice agreements with Egypt, Jordan, Lebanon, and Syria. However, there were no formal peace treaties, because the Arab nations refused to officially recognize Israel's existence. As a result of the war, more than 700,000 Palestinian Arabs fled or were driven out of Israel and became refugees. Most of them ended up in Jordan, including the West Bank, or the Gaza Strip. Some went to Lebanon and Syria. But about 150,000 remained in the territory gained by Israel.

Meir served as minister of labor from 1949 to 1956. In her autobiography, she recalled this period as "the most satisfying and happiest of my life."[7] Her biggest challenge was to provide for the enormous surge of immigrants. Because the tasks for the job had not yet been determined, she focused on food, housing, medical care, education, and jobs for the many refugees. Meir later noted that 684,201 Jews from 70 countries arrived in Israel between its independence and the end of 1951. Many of these early immigrants were refugees who arrived with little to nothing. On May 24, 1949, Meir presented a housing plan to the Knesset that called for construction of 30,000 one-room housing units. She secured funding for them from Jews in the United States. The housing project provided not only shelter for those who would live in the units but also jobs for immigrants in constructing them. Meir personally conducted numerous inspection tours to monitor the progress of the project. In late summer, she introduced another program, this time to build a network of roads throughout Israel to help the country become more interconnected. Despite the generosity of the Americans and others, it was difficult for Israel to raise enough money to finance these massive early development efforts along with the needed expenditures for maintaining the nation's strong defense. The armistice agreements notwithstanding, no one in the Israeli government believed that conflicts with the Arabs were over. By the end of 1949, Israel's population had reached 1 million. Rationing of food and clothing, including shoes, became necessary in the early 1950's. For the most part, the Jewish people—many of whom had endured far greater hardships elsewhere before they arrived in Israel—accepted these temporary sacrifices for the growth of the new nation. To avoid overreliance on foreign charity, Meir, American financier Henry Montor, and Eliezer Kaplan, Israel's minister of finance at that time, discussed a new way of raising funds: selling bonds. The first Israel bond campaign, launched in May 1951, was a huge success. This

Meir served as Israel's minister of labor from 1949 to 1956. She is shown speaking before the United Nations Political Committee in 1953 as Israel's delegate.

new financial strategy helped stabilize the nation's economy. By 1952, the flow of immigrants began to subside. In January 1952, Meir presented a bill in the Knesset to establish national health insurance. This bill led to the passage of the National Insurance Act in 1954.

INTERNAL CONFLICTS
WITHIN THE NEW NATION

In late 1953, Ben-Gurion resigned his dual position as prime minister and minister of defense and temporarily retired to a kibbutz in the Negev Desert region in southern Israel. At 67, the "Old Man," as he was nicknamed, had grown weary and decided to take a two-year sabbatical for the sake of his declining health. Meir was among those in the government who begged him to stay, but he would not be dissuaded. The Mapai chose Moshe Sharett, Israel's minister of foreign affairs, to succeed Ben-Gurion as prime minister. Ben-Gurion's handpicked successor as minister of defense was Pinchas Lavon. Meir and others thought Lavon lacked both the experience and the judgment for that key position, but Ben-Gurion refused to budge from his choice. The haughty Lavon proved to be difficult to work with and disrespectful of Sharett. Meir and fellow Mapai leaders Levi Eshkol and Zalman Aranne visited Ben-Gurion at the kibbutz in the summer of 1954 to complain about the tensions caused by Lavon. But Ben-Gurion's only advice was that Eshkol, who was then minister of finance, have a talk with Lavon. That year, a scandal erupted when Egyptian security services captured a group of Israeli-trained Egyptian Jews who were trying to set off firebombs at American and British facilities in Alexandria and Cairo. The sabotage was intended to evoke anti-Egyptian sentiment and to suggest that the new Egyptian regime was incapable of maintaining order. Some Israelis feared that, should the British leave the Suez Canal zone as had been announced, the Egyptians would become more aggressive. Furthermore, Egypt had approached the United States for arms assistance and there was fear of reduced American support for Israel. The incident was a major embarrassment to Prime Minister Sharett, whose government had not been consulted before the plan was put into effect. However, Col. Binyamin Gibli, the head of Israeli military intelligence, insisted that he had received orders from Lavon to carry out the mission. Lavon denied Gibli's claim and accused Gibli of planning the operation behind his back. Sharett appointed a committee of inquiry to investigate, but it could not reach a conclusion regarding the affair. Lavon was forced to resign, and Gibli was assigned to another post. The whole affair was hushed up and not known publicly at the time. As a result of Lavon's resignation, Ben-Gurion was summoned back to the government and reinstated as minister of defense on Feb. 21, 1955.

Parliamentary elections were held in July 1955. The Mapai won a majority of the Knesset seats and chose to make Ben-Gurion prime minister again in addition to his position as defense minister. Sharett then became minister of foreign affairs. The two men's contrasting personalities—Ben-Gurion was a forceful fighter, Sharett a diplomatic negotiator—had complemented one another in an effective way during the early growth of the new nation. However, by the mid-1950's, their differences in style contributed to disagreements over foreign policy that impaired the smooth operation of the government and weakened the power of the Mapai. At a party meeting in 1956, when Sharett jokingly suggested that he take over leadership of the Mapai, Ben-Gurion jumped at the opportunity for a face-saving way to relieve Sharett of his position as foreign minister. Soon afterward, over her own objections, Ben-Gurion chose Meir as minister of foreign affairs in June 1956. He would later reportedly call her "the only man in my cabinet."[8] When she became foreign minister, Meir felt she could no longer avoid following Ben-Gurion's long-standing belief that citizens of Israel should have Hebrew names. Ben-Gurion himself had changed his original last name of Green soon after his arrival in Palestine from Russia as a Zionist pioneer in the early 1900's. Others in Ben-Gurion's cabinet had followed suit after the State of Israel came into existence. She altered her married last name of Meyerson to *Meir*, meaning *illuminate*.

Meir served as minister of foreign affairs from 1956 to 1966. She assumed the post at a critical time. Border clashes between Arab and Israeli troops had been occurring frequently since the early 1950's.

Meir was Israel's minister of foreign affairs when she was photographed casting her vote in Israel's 1959 election.

Such clashes escalated in the mid-1950's after Egypt started giving financial aid and military supplies to Palestinian Arab *fedayeen* (commandos). The fedayeen raided Israel from the Egyptian-occupied Gaza Strip. Israeli forces then raided the Gaza Strip in return. Egypt also prevented Israeli ships from using the Suez Canal and halted them at the entrance to the Gulf of Aqaba. The Suez Canal—a narrow, artificial waterway about 100 miles (160 kilometers) long—links the Mediterranean and Red seas and serves as a key shipping route between Europe and Asia. The canal is located in Egypt but at that time was operated by the Suez Canal Company, an international firm owned mainly by the British and French. In accordance with a 1954 agreement with Egypt, the British troops that had been guarding the Suez Canal left the canal zone in June 1956. In July, the United Kingdom and the United States withdrew their offers to help finance construction of the Aswan High Dam across the Nile River. The dam was designed to control the floodwaters of the Nile and to provide Egypt with a year-round supply of water for irrigation. U.S. interest in the dam stemmed from concern over possible Communist expansion in the area by the Soviet Union and its allies. The Americans and British canceled their financing offers after Egypt solicited aid for the dam and bought arms from Communists. Anger over the withdrawal of support for this important dam, fueled by a strong Egyptian nationalist movement, led Egyptian President Gamal Abdel Nasser to *nationalize* (take control of) the Suez Canal Company on July 26. He planned to use the canal tolls to finance the building of the dam. Although Israel joined many other nations in condemning Nasser's seizure of the canal, Meir was more concerned that this action could be part of a larger Arab plan to attack Israel in the near future. On Ben-Gurion's orders, Meir was a member of an Israeli delegation that traveled to France in September for the first in a series of secret meetings with French and British representatives plotting a way to end Egypt's control of the Suez Canal. On October 29, Israeli forces invaded Egypt's Sinai Peninsula—a large, dry land area that lies between Israel and the Suez

Canal—and quickly defeated the Egyptian forces there. The United Kingdom and France publicly demanded that both Israel and Egypt withdraw from the canal zone and allow a joint British-French force to occupy the area. Neither nation complied. On October 31, the United Kingdom and France launched air strikes against Egypt. By November 5, Israeli forces occupied the Gaza Strip as well as the Sinai Peninsula, and the British and French held key ports and controlled the northern entrance to the Suez Canal. Under threat of armed intervention from the Soviet Union, which had protested the invasion along with the United States and other nations, the United Kingdom and France agreed to a UN-sponsored cease-fire on November 6, and the fighting stopped. A UN peacekeeping force was sent to Egypt.

With the military battle of the Suez crisis over, the diplomatic battle began. In December 1956, as the UN peacekeeping force finished evacuating the British and French troops from Egypt, Meir went to New York City to address the United Nations. Speaking before the UN General Assembly on December 5, she said:

> The fundamental problem in the whole situation is the systematically organized Arab hostility against Israel. This Arab enmity is not a natural phenomenon. It is artificially fostered and nurtured. It is not, as been alleged here, Israel which is an instrument of colonialism. It is the Israel-Arab conflict which keeps the area at the mercy of dangerously contending outside forces. Only by the liquidation of that conflict will the people of the region be able to work out their own destinies in independence and hope. Only in that prospect lies hope for a brighter future of equality and progress for all the peoples concerned. If hatred is abandoned as a principle of Arab policies, everything becomes possible.
>
> Over and over again the Israeli government has held out its hand in peace to its neighbors. But to no avail. . . . Our offer to meet the representatives of all or any of the Arab countries still stands. . . .
>
> Can we envisage what a state of peace between Israel and its neighbors during the past eight years would have meant for all of us? Can we try to translate fighter planes into irrigation pipes and tractors for the people in these lands? Can we, in our imagination, replace gun emplacements by schools and hospitals? The many

hundreds of millions of dollars spent on armaments could surely have been put to a more constructive purpose.

Substitute cooperation between Israel and its neighbors for sterile hatred and ardor for destruction, and you will give life and hope and happiness to all its people.[9]

But Meir's appeal did not sway her audience this time. Over the next several months, she met a number of times with U.S. Secretary of State John Foster Dulles and U.S. Ambassador to the United Nations Henry Cabot Lodge to reach some sort of compromise regarding the withdrawal of Israeli forces from Egypt. After receiving an assurance of support from Dulles that UN forces would remain in control, Meir made a statement before the UN General Assembly on March 3, 1957, announcing Israel's planned withdrawal from the Sinai Peninsula and the Gaza Strip. But when Lodge stood and spoke, he did not offer the promised support. Instead, he said that the future of the Gaza Strip should be worked out within the framework of the armistice agreements, which meant that control of the strip would revert to Egypt. Meir was dismayed at this betrayal, and Ben-Gurion was furious. Later that month, Israeli forces completed their phased withdrawal from the Sinai, but they took a measure of revenge by ripping up highways, railroad tracks, and telephone poles as they went. Later that spring, the Suez Canal reopened under Egyptian management.

Meir continued throughout her tenure as foreign minister to approach Arab delegates at the UN, even in such informal ways as meeting for a cup of coffee. But she found that most Arabs would not even stay in the same room with her, let alone talk to her. However, Meir enjoyed some success in the late 1950's and early 1960's in her efforts to establish closer ties between Israel and many of the newly independent nations in Africa. Eager to share the young nation's experiences in economic and social development, she traveled to developing countries and offered practical advice on how to build a modern infrastructure of roads, sanitation systems, and housing for a growing population and how to establish such important social services as medical care and education. When she talked about setting up collective farms, it was with the voice of experience. She set up programs under which African workers could receive training in Israel and then return to their homelands to put it to use. She also sent Israeli engineers, teachers, and others to help develop African communities. In her numerous trips to Africa, Meir enjoyed getting away from meetings with government officials and touring the countryside, chatting with the people she encountered. She once let a dozen little girls in Ghana take turns brushing her hair, the length and texture of which fascinated them. Meir also made trips to Asia and South America that helped strengthen Israel's position internationally.

PARTY LEADER

Meir's loyalty to Ben-Gurion wavered in the early 1960's. Although she had been given free rein in Africa, Ben-Gurion himself directed Israel's foreign relations with the United States and the European nations. Meir began to feel that she was not being trusted to do her job as foreign minister and was being kept in the position just for show. Within the Mapai, Meir was among those who disagreed with Ben-Gurion's attempts to bring certain young men he favored, including Shimon Peres and Moshe Dayan, into the party and promote them to important government positions without the support of the Mapai's long-time members. Ben-Gurion also had maintained cordial relations with the disgraced Pinchas Lavon, whom he had managed to return to a position of power as head of the Histadrut in 1955. Lavon, unwilling to let the earlier affair drop, demanded a public exoneration from Ben-Gurion in 1960 after new evidence was brought forward to support his initial claim that he had not ordered the 1954 acts of sabotage in Egypt. Ben-Gurion refused, on the grounds that he personally had not accused Lavon of anything and that only a court of law could clear him.

Israeli foreign minister Meir made goodwill visits to several South Asian countries. She is shown shaking hands with Philippine president Diosdado Macapagal in Manila in 1962.

David Ben-Gurion and foreign minister Meir are seated at the cabinet table at the Knesset, Israel's parliament in Tel Aviv, in 1963.

In an effort to quietly resolve the issue, Finance Minister Eshkol asked Justice Minister Pinhas Rosen to lead a committee of seven government ministers to determine the legal procedures for handling the matter. Ben-Gurion had insisted that a judicial inquiry be launched. In the meantime, Lavon indirectly leaked word of the situation to the press, so the whole messy business became public. The committee subsequently decided in Lavon's favor. Ben-Gurion then hinted he would resign if Lavon did not give up his Histadrut position. Shortly afterward, in 1961, the Mapai leadership ousted Lavon. However, the scandal, which became known as the Lavon Affair, damaged the Mapai and estranged Ben-Gurion from Meir, Eshkol, and other ministers who felt they had been severely mistreated by him. On June 16, 1963, Ben-Gurion resigned as prime minister. Eshkol succeeded him. Meir stayed on as minister of foreign affairs.

The 1965 parliamentary election campaign left the 67-year-old Meir exhausted. During her nine years as foreign minister, she had been working 18-hour days, and the pace was catching up with her. She had also suffered a number of health problems over the years, including gall-bladder attacks in the mid-1940's for which she had surgery in 1953; a broken leg in 1948; a dislocated shoulder in the early 1950's; and a leg injury incurred in an explosion after a grenade was thrown at the table in the Knesset where she and other government leaders were sitting on the one-year anniversary of the Sinai invasion, Oct. 29, 1957. But even more than her physical health, Meir felt a need to "recharge my emotional batteries, which seemed to be running down because I was tired."[10] Prime Minister Eshkol tried to dissuade her from her intention to resign from his cabinet, even offering her the post of deputy prime minister, but Meir declined. As she later reflected, "Better, I thought, to be a full-time grandmother than a part-time minister, and I told Eshkol that I really wanted to retire."[11] She resigned as minister of foreign affairs in January 1966. Abba Eban succeeded her.

Meir was glad to have the freedom to spend more time with her five grandchildren—three of whom were born to Menachem, two to Sarah—and with both sisters. She also enjoyed the simple pleasures of taking walks, riding the bus, doing her own shopping, cooking, cleaning house, and reading books. She remained a member of the Knesset and the Mapai Executive but did no more than she felt like doing for them. But this blissful existence would not last for long.

PARTY LEADER

After the 1965 parliamentary elections, the weakened Mapai rejoined with Ahdut Haavoda—one of the two parties from which the Mapai was originally formed but which had split off from the Mapai in 1944—to form an alignment. But the alignment was still weaker than the old Mapai had been before the resignation of Ben-Gurion. The disenchanted Old Man and a group of his followers had subsequently broken off from the Mapai to form their own party, the Rafi. Prime Minister Eshkol, concerned about the future of Israel's labor movement, sought to unify the country's labor interests into a single labor party. And he thought Meir was the one who could do it. At Eshkol's request, Meir reluctantly came out of retirement to undertake the task. She was named secretary-general of Mapai in 1966. In her role as party leader, Meir became one of Eshkol's closest advisers.

In May 1967, in response to Egyptian President Nasser's demands, the UN removed its peacekeeping force from the Sinai Peninsula and the Gaza Strip. Then—just as Meir expected would happen—Nasser sent massive numbers of troops into the Sinai. He also announced the closure to Israeli shipping of the Strait of Tiran leading into the Gulf of Aqaba, which would block the Israeli port of Elat and cut off Israel's only access to the Red Sea. By June 5, Egypt had signed defense agreements with Syria, Jordan, and Iraq to create a joint military command. Israel considered these Arab actions preparations for war and decided not to wait for the attack it believed was inevitable. On June 5, Israeli forces launched a surprise air attack against Egypt. Syria, Jordan, and Iraq immediately joined Egypt in the fighting. But within hours, the Israeli warplanes destroyed nearly all of the Arab air forces. Then Israeli tanks advanced into the Sinai Peninsula, and Israel's ground forces defeated those of the Arab states. By the time a UN cease-fire ended the fighting six days later, on June 10, Israel had captured the Sinai Peninsula, the Gaza Strip, the West Bank, the eastern half of Jerusalem, and the Golan Heights, a region of Syria bordering Israel. Israel vowed to keep occupying these territories until the Arab states officially recognized Israel's right to exist. Without this basic recognition, Meir and other Israeli leaders believed, peace in the Middle East would not be possible, and they thought that perhaps Israel's decisive victory in the war would convince the Arabs to negotiate peaceful coexistence. The Six-Day War, as it became known in Israel, brought about 1 million hostile Arabs living in the West Bank and Gaza Strip under Israeli control. The fate of these Palestinian Arabs played a large role in the Arab-Israeli struggle after the war.

After the war, Meir returned to the assignment that had brought her out of retirement. Following months of negotiation, she was able to persuade Rafi to merge into the new party. The Israel Labor Party was officially formed on Jan. 21, 1968, and still exists today. Meir was named head of the new Labor Party. By the end of the summer, though she remained party head, she considered herself retired and once more retreated into private life. The retirement would not last for long this time, either.

Chapter 5: Prime Minister

Golda Meir was alone at her home in Tel Aviv on Feb. 26, 1969, when she received a phone call informing her that Israeli Prime Minister Levi Eshkol had suffered a heart attack and died. Meir was shocked. She had talked with him only the night before, and nothing had seemed wrong. They had even planned to meet two days later. Meir considered Eshkol a dear friend as well as a valued colleague in the government, and the loss grieved her. She went to Jerusalem and waited for an emergency cabinet meeting to end so that she could find out about the funeral arrangements. After the meeting, Deputy Prime Minister Yigal Allon became acting prime minister. However, within the Labor Party, Allon, a former member of Ahdut Haavoda, was the chief rival of defense minister and former Rafi leader Moshe Dayan. Fearing that a factional split might result if either of these men were named prime minister, Labor leaders looked for someone else who would be more acceptable to everyone in the party, someone with experience in government, someone respected by the public. It had to be Golda Meir.

The 70-year-old Meir, content in her retirement, was surprised to be asked to assume such an important position at this stage in her life. She knew the stress of the responsibility would be enormous. When she asked her son and daughter for their opinions, they understood her concern but agreed with the party leaders that having her as prime minister would be in the best interest of the nation. She consented, and on March 7, the Central Committee of the Labor Party voted in favor of nominating Meir as prime minister. She was duly appointed by President Zalman Shazar and sworn into office on March 17. Meir retained Dayan, who had abstained from the vote for her, as minister of defense. Allon resumed the position of deputy prime minister and was also named minister of education and culture.

Meir came out of retirement in 1969 to serve as Israel's prime minister. She is shown with Zalman Shazar, who served as president of Israel from 1963 to 1973.

Parliamentary elections were held in late October 1969. The Labor Party won a majority, and Meir remained prime minister.

CHALLENGES AND ACCOMPLISHMENTS

As prime minister, Meir worked to strengthen Israel's relations with the United States. In late September 1969, she visited U.S. President Richard Nixon in Washington, D.C., for several days of productive meetings, capped by a state dinner in her honor. Guests at the dinner included numerous high-ranking politicians and dignitaries along with Meir's son and his family, who lived in the United States at that time, and Israel's ambassador to the United States, Yitzhak Rabin. This trip and subsequent visits helped Meir develop a cordial relationship with Nixon that made her feel more secure about U.S. support for Israel. Low-interest loans and other forms of U.S. aid bolstered Israel's economy in the early 1970's, and the American military aircraft that Israel was able to buy helped the Israel Defense Forces (IDF) during later fighting between Israel and the surrounding Arab nations.

The territorial conflict between Israel and the Arab nations of the region was the most challenging issue Meir faced as prime minister. She followed a firm policy toward the Arabs, but she never gave up hope that peace with them could be achieved. Peace did not seem likely, however, while Gamal Abdel Nasser remained president of Egypt. After Egypt's defeat in the Six-Day War, Egyptian and Israeli forces continued to engage in clashes along the western border of the Sinai Peninsula. Nasser relied heavily on Soviet military assistance. The fighting intensified between April 1969 and August 1970, when it was ended by a U.S.-sponsored cease-fire. Nasser agreed to a 90-day cease-fire. However, Nasser died on

Meir's popularity in the United States is evidenced by this group of children greeting the Israeli prime minister as she arrives at the Philadelphia airport in 1969.

Sept. 28, 1970, and the cease-fire lasted longer than 90 days. Nasser's successor was Anwar el-Sadat. In her autobiography, Meir recalled her feelings about the prospects for peace under Sadat:

> Not only did Sadat seem, at first glance, to be a more reasonable man who might soberly consider the benefits of an end to the war to his own people but there were also indications that he wasn't getting along too well with the Russians. And in Jordan, King Hussein, having happily sheltered the Palestinian terrorists for months, suddenly found himself so threatened by them that in September he turned on them and crushed them. . . . The Arab leaders didn't modify their statements about Israel in any way or alter their demands for a total withdrawal of our troops, but there was talk about reopening the Suez Canal [which was blocked by sunken ships from the 1967 war] and rebuilding the ruined Egyptian towns along its banks, so that normal life could be restored in them—all of which gave rise to some optimism in Israel. Well, the cease-fire held, we stayed where we were, the Arabs continued to refuse to meet us or deal with us in any way, and the optimism in Israel slowly died down—but it didn't vanish altogether, and war didn't break out in 1971 or 1972! But neither did peace . . .[1]

This impasse continued into 1973. Meir made several trips abroad that year. On January 15, she became the first Israeli prime minister to meet with the pope, the head of the Roman Catholic

President Richard M. Nixon welcomes Meir on the South Lawn of the White House on her first official visit to the United States as prime minister in September 1969. Meir developed a cordial relationship with Nixon that made her feel more secure about U.S. support for Israel.

Pope Paul VI received Prime Minister Meir at the Vatican Palace in 1973. Although Vatican City had not officially recognized the existence of Israel, the pope was interested in discussing the situation in the Middle East with Meir.

Church. Pope Paul VI received her at the Vatican Palace in Vatican City, an independent country located within the city of Rome. Vatican City had not yet officially recognized the existence of Israel, but the pope was interested in discussing the situation in the Middle East. Roman Catholics and other Christians consider Jerusalem a holy place because many events in the life of Jesus Christ occurred in and around the city. The pope, who was accustomed to deferential treatment by his visitors, was taken aback at first by Meir's frankness, but their conversation was cordial overall and left open the possibility for further dialogue between Israel and the Vatican in the future. In March, Meir revisited U.S. President Nixon in Washington, D.C. Shortly before this visit, Israeli warplanes shot down a Libyan plane that had flown off course and entered the airspace over the Sinai Peninsula that they were guarding. Israeli intelligence sources earlier had warned the Israel Defense Forces of a possible suicide attack by terrorists attempting to land a plane loaded with explosives, and when the pilot of the Libyan plane refused to identify himself, the Israeli fighters fired on it. What the fighters did not know was that the plane had been carrying passengers, and 106 people on the plane were killed. Nixon was sympathetic to Meir's explanation of the incident.

THE YOM KIPPUR WAR

In May 1973, Israeli intelligence sources received information that Egypt and Syria were building up their troops along those countries' borders with Israel. Defense Minister Dayan and IDF Chief of Staff David "Dado" Elazar reported to Meir that Israel's armed forces were prepared for war if necessary. But Egypt and Syria took no further action then. In September, intelligence reports about a buildup of Syrian troops in the Golan Heights began to filter in. Israeli warplanes downed 13 Syrian military jets in an air skirmish on September 13. Syria continued to reinforce its troops, and Egypt resumed its earlier buildup of forces near the Sinai Peninsula, but Meir's intelligence staff repeatedly assured her that the buildup was only in anticipation of defending against a possible Israeli attack, not for aggressive purposes. On October 3, a Wednesday, Meir held a meeting that included Allon, Dayan, Elazar and several other military leaders, and Yisrael Galili, a minister without portfolio who was a trusted member of her cabinet. These advisers were disturbed by the Syrian and Egyptian actions but also had reasonable explanations for them. None of the advisers believed that war was imminent and thus felt there was no need to call up Israel's reserve defense forces at that time. Yom Kippur, the holiest day in Judaism, would begin that Friday evening, October 5, and many soldiers had been granted leave to be home with their families for the weekend. Nearly all businesses and public services in the country would be shut down from sunset on Friday until sunset on Saturday, October 6, in observance of the holiday, during which Jews would fast and pray. Meir scheduled a cabinet meeting for Sunday, October 7, at which she and her advisers would discuss the situation further. In her autobiography, Meir recalled what happened next:

> On [the morning of] Friday, October 5, we received a report that worried me. The families of the Russian advisers in Syria were packing up and leaving in a hurry. It reminded me of what had happened prior to the Six-Day War, and I didn't like it at all. Why the haste? What did those Russian families know that we didn't know? Was it possible that they were being evacuated? In all the welter of

information pouring into my office that one little detail had taken
root in my mind, and I couldn't shake myself free of it. But since
no one around me seemed very perturbed about it, I tried not to
become obsessive. Besides, intuition is a very tricky thing; some-
times it must be acted on at once, but sometimes it is merely a
symptom of anxiety and then it can be very misleading indeed.[2]

Meir would later deeply regret that she did not act more boldly on her intuition that morning. She convened an emergency cabinet meeting at noon in which she expressed her fears. The cabinet
passed a resolution to bypass its usual procedure requiring a cabinet vote to authorize calling up the reserves and instead allow
Meir and Dayan alone to make that decision if necessary. Meir
also suggested contacting the United States to report what was
going on in the hope that the Americans would pressure the
Soviets to dissuade the Syrians from any aggressive action against
Israel. Dayan and Elazar thought there was no need to call up the
reserves at that point. They assured Meir that the armed forces
had been placed on high alert and that they would receive ade-
quate warning if any serious trouble developed. But Meir
remained uneasy. She joined her son's family for dinner before sunset and then went to bed, but she lay awake for hours before drift-
ing off to sleep.

At about 4:00 a.m. on Saturday, October 6, Meir received a
telephone call from her military secretary, Yisrael Lior. He reported that intelligence sources had reliable information indicating
that Syria and Egypt would launch an attack against Israel late
that afternoon. She ordered Lior to summon Allon, Dayan, Elazar,
and Galili to her office by 7:00 a.m. and quickly arrived there herself. By 8:00 a.m., Dayan and Elazar were arguing over which
reserve divisions to call up and how soon. She followed Elazar's
recommendation to immediately call up four army divisions and
the entire air force reserve. These forces would be mobilized and
ready for action the next day. Elazar further recommended that
Israeli strike forces be ordered to attack first, but Meir remem-
bered the criticism Israel had received from other nations for its
preemptive strike in the Six-Day War. If Israel struck first this time,

she believed, then it might not get the support it needed once the war was underway. She called the U.S. ambassador to Israel, Kenneth Keating, to inform him that Israel expected to be attacked within hours but would not strike first, still desperately hoping for American intervention to prevent the war.

Meir convened an emergency cabinet meeting at noon. As she reported to her ministers on the events of the morning, Lior burst into the room to announce that the shooting had started, and air raid sirens went off. The war had started even earlier than anticipated. Israeli forces scrambled to respond. Syria and Egypt had launched a simultaneous assault. In the north, Syrian forces pushed Israeli troops from the Golan Heights. In the south, Egyptian forces attacked Israeli positions along the Suez Canal. Israel suffered heavy losses of soldiers and equipment at the beginning of the war. But by October 10, Israeli forces had begun to push the Arab forces back. On October 14, the first of many shipments of U.S. warplanes and other military equipment arrived. By October 24, Israeli forces had crossed the Suez Canal and surrounded the Egyptian army. They also recaptured the Golan

Israeli forces make their way to the northernmost stronghold along the Suez Canal in North Sinai during the Yom Kippur War in October 1973. The war had lasting effects, both domestically and internationally.

Heights and some additional Syrian territory. A cease-fire went into effect on October 24.

The Yom Kippur War, as it became known in Israel, because the attack occurred on the sacred Jewish holy day, had lasting effects, both domestically and internationally. At home, the Israeli economy suffered greatly from the expense of the war. And though Israel won the war, many Israelis criticized their government's handling of the conflict. In the international arena, the war greatly increased Israel's dependence on the United States, but it also drew U.S. attention to the need for stability in the Middle East. Despite its ultimate failure, Egyptian President Sadat's bold assault on Israel raised his popularity among Arabs and made him a powerful world leader. As a result, he was able to pursue his goal of negotiating with Israel to end the long-standing conflict between the two nations. As a first step, Israel and Egypt agreed to a separation of their forces in the Sinai in 1974.

Meir was left with a lingering sense of regret. In her autobiography, she reflected:

> *That Friday morning [Oct. 5, 1973] I should have listened to the warnings of my own heart and ordered a callup. . . . It doesn't matter what logic dictated. It matters only that I, who was so accustomed to making decisions—and who did make them throughout the war—failed to make that one decision. . . . I shall live with that terrible knowledge for the rest of my life.*[3]

Some Israeli voters were apparently more forgiving of Meir than she was of herself. Parliamentary elections, originally scheduled for late October but postponed because of the war, were held on Dec. 31, 1973. The Labor Party emerged with more votes than any other party, but its margin of victory had narrowed since the last election. It would have to form a coalition to run the government. Meir remained prime minister. On April 1, 1974, the initial report published by a commission investigating the Yom Kippur War cleared both Meir and Dayan of any wrongdoing, although it was so critical of Elazar that he immediately resigned. For Meir, the burden of leadership had grown too heavy. On April 11, she announced her resignation to the Labor Party. On April 22, the

party elected her successor: Yitzhak Rabin, the former Israeli ambassador to the United States, who had been elected to the Knesset for the first time in the most recent election. Meir remained in office until Rabin received a vote of approval from the Knesset on June 2. Rabin formed a coalition government led by the Labor Party.

At the age of 77, Golda Meir retired for the last time. She returned to her home in Tel Aviv and resumed nonpolitical activities that she enjoyed. She published her autobiography, *My Life,* in 1975, and she attended the premiere of the biographical Broadway show *Golda,* starring Anne Bancroft, in November 1977. For more than a decade, Meir suffered from lymphatic cancer, but she kept her medical condition a secret. Meir died from complications of the disease at the age of 80 on Dec. 8, 1978, in Jerusalem.

Meir was given a state funeral. She was buried near fellow former prime minister Levi Eshkol at Mount Herzl National Cemetery in west Jerusalem. In her will, Meir requested that no eulogies be delivered at her funeral and no institutions be named after her. However, the Golda Meir Library at the University of Wisconsin-Milwaukee was named for her in 1979; the Golda Meir School (formerly Fourth Street School) was named for her on May 7, 1979; and on Dec. 3, 1979, New York City dedicated the Golda

Meir Memorial Square on Broadway. In addition, the Golda Meir House, her Denver home, is now at the Metropolitan State College of Denver.

Although Meir followed a firm policy toward the Arabs, she was hopeful that peace with them could be achieved. However, the territorial conflict between Israel and several Arab countries has remained a primary concern for every Israeli prime minister since Meir. In the last decade, control of Israel's government has shifted several times between parties, resulting in an inconsistency of leadership that hindered the peace process. In 2002, Israel reoccupied most West Bank cities. But on Sept. 12, 2005, the last Israeli forces withdrew from the Gaza Strip, and the Palestinian Authority took control of the territory. In June 2006, leaders of Hamas, the militant group in control of the Palestinian parliament, agreed to sign a document creating a national unity government and endorsing a two-nation solution to the Palestinian-Israeli conflict. ■

Meir died at age 80 on Dec. 8, 1978, in Jerusalem. The former prime minister was given a state funeral.

Yitzhak Rabin (1922–1995)

Yitzhak Rabin *(YITS hahk rah BEEN)* was the first Israeli prime minister born in what is now Israel. He served as prime minister of Israel from 1974 to 1977 and again from 1992 until his assassination in 1995. A soldier initially and a politician later in his life, Rabin strove not only to maintain a strong national defense but also to promote peace in the region. For this latter effort, he won the 1994 Nobel Peace Prize. Rabin had an introverted personality but he argued passionately for the causes he believed in. Unlike many public figures—including previous Israeli prime ministers David Ben-Gurion and Golda Meir—he also placed great importance on spending time with his family and as a result enjoyed warm, close relationships with his wife, children, and grandchildren.

ZION PIONEER SON

Yitzhak Rabin was born March 1, 1922, in Jerusalem. At that time, what is now Israel was part of Palestine, which was under the control of a British *mandate* (order to rule). Rabin's parents, Nehemiah Rabin and Rosa Cohen, were among the Jewish settlers who came to Palestine in the early 1900's as part of an immigration movement called *Zionism*.

Both of Yitzhak Rabin's parents had been born in Russia during the late 1800's, a time when a revolutionary movement against the ruling *czar* (emperor) was starting. It was also a time when *pogroms (poh GROMZ or POH gruhmz)* (riots against Jews) made life difficult for Jewish families such as theirs. In response to such persecution, groups of Jewish youths in Russia calling themselves *Hoveve-Zion* (Lovers of *Zion*, the poetic Hebrew name for Palestine) started Zionism in 1882 to encourage Jewish immigration to Palestine, the ancient Jewish homeland. Rosa Cohen moved to Palestine in 1919 and quickly became an activist in the Jewish community there. Nehemiah Rabin took a more circuitous route to Palestine, immigrating first to the United States in 1905. He studied at the University of Chicago and worked as a tailor. Through the Jewish Tailors' Union, he became involved in the Jewish workers' movement *Poalei Zion* (Workers for Zion). In 1918, toward the end of World War I (1914–1918), Rabin enlisted in the Jewish Legion, a division of the British Army made up of Jewish volunteer soldiers including David Ben-Gurion, who would later become Israel's first prime minister. After his discharge from the army in 1920, Rabin went to work installing telephone lines for the British who were in Haifa, under a mandate. Rabin and Cohen met in 1920 and married in 1921. Cohen kept her own last name. Also in 1921, Cohen began to organize the Haifa branch of the *Haganah*, a secret Jewish military force that was formed after the British refused to consider establishing an official Jewish armed service in Palestine. She also held a regular job as an accountant. Cohen stayed with a cousin in Jerusalem for a few months in early 1922 in order to give birth in the Jews' holiest city, which also had the best medical facilities. She and baby Yitzhak then returned to Haifa.

In 1923, Cohen officially became commander of the Haifa Haganah. She juggled her schedule so that she could plot military strategy for the Haganah but also spend time at home nursing her baby. Later that year, the family moved to Tel Aviv so Nehemiah Rabin could work at the newly founded Palestine Electric Corporation. Cohen got an accounting job at a construction company owned by the *Histadrut* (General Federation of Labor) that Ben-Gurion had helped create. One of Cohen's co-workers at the construction company was Golda Meyerson (later Meir), a future prime minister of Israel. Cohen also was elected to the Tel Aviv City Council, where she became an outspoken advocate for working-class people. She gave birth to a second child, Rachel Rabin, on Feb. 1, 1925.

As a child, Yitzhak Rabin was an extremely shy boy with reddish-brown hair and blue eyes. From 1928 until his graduation in 1935, he attended Beit Hinuch (School for Workers' Children). His subjects included botany, geography, Hebrew, world history, and zoology. When not studying, he enjoyed playing marbles, chess, and soccer.

The students at Beit Hinuch put some of their knowledge to practical use by growing flowers and vegetables in a garden next to the school. Yitzhak also took care of a donkey at the school. At Beit Hinuch, Yitzhak studied the Bible from a cultural rather than a religious point of view. This viewpoint was reinforced at home, where his parents rejected Jewish religious practices but took great pride in their Jewish cultural heritage. Yitzhak learned about *Judaism*, the religion of the Jews, after he befriended the rabbi of a synagogue across the street from his home. With both parents working full-time and heavily involved in community activities, everyone in the family pitched in to help with the household chores.

Throughout Yitzhak's childhood, there were ongoing conflicts between Jewish immigrants and indigenous Arabs in Palestine. These conflicts sometimes trickled down to the level of the children. One day, some Arab children began throwing rocks at Yitzhak and his Jewish companions, who retaliated in kind. The skirmish ended in a draw, and Yitzhak suddenly comprehended the relevance of a teacher's lesson about the importance of Jews and Arabs learning to live together in peace.

In 1935, at the age of 13, Yitzhak enrolled in the two-year, agriculturally oriented education program at Givat Hashlosha, a school his mother had founded on a *kibbutz* (communal settlement) outside Tel Aviv. In addition to the academic subjects, he learned how to fire a pistol and received military training from the Haganah. He also joined the Jewish youth movement *Noar Ha'oved* (Working Youth). Yitzhak decided that he would concentrate on furthering his education in agricultural science so that he could spend the rest of his life working on a kibbutz.

In October 1937, after passing a rigorous and highly competitive entrance examination, Rabin started high school at the British-administered Kadouri Agricultural School in the remote, mountainous Galilee region of northern Palestine. He had barely begun his studies when he received word in November that his mother was dying. She had suffered for many years from a heart ailment but succumbed in the end to cancer. Rabin rushed home to Tel Aviv and was with his mother at the hospital when she died. He then returned to Kadouri and immersed himself in his studies. His classes included agronomy, anatomy, arithmetic, botany, chemistry, English, leadership, physics, zoology, and courses in the raising of bees, poultry, cattle, and sheep. Rabin also was captain of the school soccer team. He improved his military skills with instruction from the Haganah officer Yigal Allon. Rabin graduated on Aug. 20, 1940, winning the top prize awarded to the best student in Palestine. Rabin applied to the University of California at Berkeley with the intention of studying water engineering for irrigation. In the meantime, he went to live and work at the Ramat Yohanan kibbutz near Haifa.

THE PALMACH AND
EARLY RESISTANCE ACTIVITY

Although his application was later accepted, Rabin never made it to the university. In the spring of 1941, during World War II (1939–1945), Rabin joined the *Palmach,* the newly formed strike force of the Haganah. That summer, Rabin's unit of soldiers, under the command of Moshe Dayan, helped British forces defending Palestine by sneaking into Lebanon and literally cutting the lines of communication—telephone lines—used by the enemy. Rabin had to shinny up a telephone pole to carry out the task. That night Dayan lost his eye in a battle against the Vichy French. In late 1942, after British forces had gained the upper hand in the fighting in the Middle East, the British turned against the Haganah and attempted to disband the Palmach. The Palmach dispersed its forces to the *kibbutzim* (plural of *kibbutz*), where its members served as farmworkers and secretly continued their military activities. Although some disgruntled Palmach members resented having to perform farm labor, Rabin was delighted at this opportunity to combine his agricultural and military interests for the good of the Jewish state he was helping to build. In 1943, with additional training in sabotage and demolition, he served in a tactical unit defending Palestine. He soon rose to the rank of deputy commander of the Palmach's first battalion.

In 1945, Rabin was a key leader in a daring raid to free about 200 Jewish refugees from a British detention camp at Athlit, south of Haifa. The refugees had entered Palestine on foot from Syria in defiance of strict limitations on immigration imposed by the British, who intended to deport them. These refugees were survivors of the *Holocaust*—the Nazi campaign of systematic, state-sponsored murder during World War II that wiped out more than two-thirds of the Jews in Europe, a total of about 6 million Jewish men, women, and children. The refugees' homes had been destroyed in the war, and they did not want to be sent back to nations where they would have to live among the former killers of their people. Rabin was determined to save them from that fate.

On the night of Oct. 10, 1945, he led a Palmach assault force of about 200 members that stealthily approached the refugees' detention camp. A small group disguised as teachers and welfare workers went in first to overpower the Arab police guarding the camp and gather the detainees. Then the remaining Palmach forces advanced to escort the group on a 2-mile (3.2-kilometer) hike from the camp to the trucks that were waiting along the main road running between Haifa and Tel Aviv to take them to safety at the Yagur kibbutz. The group had to move quickly and quietly to avoid waking the British soldiers sleeping at a nearby army base. Only about half the refugees had reached the trucks when British troops arrived in an army vehicle and opened fire. Palmach forces returned fire, and the refugees who had boarded the trucks escaped unscathed. The Palmach battalion commander then sent the rest of the trucks away empty with the British in hot pursuit. Meanwhile, Rabin's unit led the remaining refugees on foot up the side of Mount Carmel to the Bet Oren kibbutz. Upon arrival shortly after dawn, they found the kibbutz surrounded by British troops. Rabin's forces nevertheless managed to sneak the refugees in through a small gap in the British defense perimeter. Once the British realized that the refugees had gotten inside, they were contemplating an attack on the kibbutz when thousands of people from Haifa, who had been organized by the Haganah, came streaming into the settlement, making it impossible for the British to distinguish the refugees amid all the others. The British gave up, and the refugees stayed in Palestine.

Rabin graduated from the British-administered Kadouri Agricultural School in Galilee in 1940, winning the top prize awarded to the best student in Palestine.

Rabin earned high praise for the success of the mission. However, for several more years, a British naval blockade prevented many ships carrying thousands of other Jewish immigrants from reaching Palestine. Zionists, including the Haganah and Palmach, continued their guerrilla tactics against the British in their ongoing struggle for an independent Jewish homeland.

In early June 1946, Rabin suffered a broken leg in a motorcycle accident while carrying out a Palmach assignment. On June 29, Rabin and his father were among about 3,000 Jewish leaders rounded up from kibbutzim throughout the area and taken to a British prison camp. Nehemiah Rabin was released within a few weeks, but Yitzhak Rabin was held for about six months. The stint in prison did not deter Yitzhak Rabin from returning to his resistance activities, however, and he was appointed deputy commander of the Palmach in October 1947. Yigal Allon was commander.

By 1947, the ruling British were exasperated with the situation in Palestine. The Zionists continued to defy the British immigration restrictions at every opportunity, but the British knew from experience that allowing unrestricted Jewish immigration would likely spark violent protests from Palestinian Arabs who made up the majority of the population. A wave of more than 100,000 Jewish refugees from Poland and Nazi Germany had flooded into Palestine in the early 1930's—an influx that alarmed the Arabs, who in turn attacked Jewish settlements and also rioted against the British in the late 1930's for allowing in so many Jews. In 1947, the United Kingdom submitted the issue to the United Nations (UN), an organization of nations formed after World War II to work for world peace and security. On November 29, the UN General Assembly adopted a plan to place Jerusalem under international control and divide the rest of Palestine into an Arab state and a Jewish state after the withdrawal of the British no later than Aug. 1, 1948. The Jews in Palestine accepted the UN decision, but the Arabs rejected it. Fighting broke out immediately. Rabin knew that a bloody struggle lay ahead.

Throughout the rest of 1947 and into 1948, the Arabs stepped up their attacks on Jewish settlements and supply convoys. David Ben-Gurion, as chairman of the Executive of the Jewish Agency, directed all Jewish affairs in Palestine and organized the defense efforts against the attacks. In the spring of 1948, Ben-Gurion ordered Haganah and Palmach forces to capture Arab strongholds along the road into Jerusalem, which had been cut off from the outside world by Arab attacks. Ben-Gurion chose Rabin to head this military operation, which succeeded in reopening the road.

On May 14, 1948, Rabin was among the thousands of people listening to the radio broadcast in which Ben-Gurion publicly read the Proclamation of Independence that declared the existence of the State of Israel. The British withdrew, and Ben-Gurion became head of the new nation's government as its first prime minister. On May 15, as Ben-Gurion had expected, neighboring Arab nations attacked Israel. The Palmach and other armed groups defended the country. On May 26, the Israeli government approved the creation of the Israel Defense Forces (IDF) as the nation's sole armed service. The IDF was to incorporate the three main Jewish resistance groups: the Haganah; the Irgun Zvai Leumi (National Military Organization), or Etzel, led by Menachem Begin; and the Lohamei Herut Yisrael (Fighters for the Freedom of Israel), also known as Lehi or the Stern Gang. In the first few months of fighting, the greatly outnumbered Jewish forces sustained heavy losses but for the most part managed to hold off the Arab attackers. During the summer and early fall, two cease-fire periods temporarily brought a halt to the fighting.

MARRIAGE AND MILITARY CAREER

On Aug. 23, 1948, during the second cease-fire, Rabin married Leah Schlossberg, a German-born Jewish émigré who grew up in a wealthy Zionist family that relocated to Palestine in 1933 after the Nazis came to power. The couple's first encounter was in 1944 at an ice-cream parlor in Tel Aviv, where their eyes met but they did not speak to one another. But the 15-year-old Leah was immediately smitten by the 21-year-old Yitzhak, whose appearance and bearing she likened to that of the biblical King David. When she encountered him on the street a few days later, she boldly struck up a conversation with him, and he was charmed by her friendly smile and outgoing personality. In 1945, after graduating from high school, Schlossberg enlisted in the Palmach and joined the battalion under Yitzhak's command. After they married, they moved in with Leah's parents, who lived in an apartment in Tel Aviv. The Rabins would later have two children: a daughter, Dalia, born March 19, 1950; and a son, Yuval, born June 18, 1955. Much later, there would be three grandchildren: Jonathan, Noa, and Michael.

Yitzhak Rabin was called back to his military duties soon after his wedding. He was promoted to the rank of colonel and sent to southern Israel to lead forces fighting against Egypt in the Negev Desert region. By August 1949, Israel and the Arab states had agreed to end the fighting. Armistice agreements were signed between Israel and Egypt, Syria, Jordan, and Lebanon. Rabin was a military representative with the Israeli delegation that attended the conference in which the armistice agreements were negotiated. There were no formal peace treaties because the Arab nations refused to officially recognize Israel's existence.

Rabin rose steadily through the ranks of the Israel Defense Forces in the 1950's and 1960's. He was head of the IDF tactical operations division from 1950 to 1952. In late 1952, accompanied by his wife and daughter, he went to Camberley, England, near London, for a year-long officer-training program at the Royal Staff College (now Joint Services Command and Staff College). He also spent several hours a day learning English. The family enjoyed the greater amount of time they had together during their stay. From 1953 to 1956, Rabin headed the IDF training branch. In the summer of 1954, Rabin was sent to the United States for a firsthand look at American military training methods. He incorporated some of his observations from that trip into an effective new training program he developed for IDF soldiers. By 1956, Rabin had reached the rank of major general. From 1956 to 1959, he was commanding officer of the IDF northern command. As such, he was not involved in the Arab-Israeli war of 1956 that centered around the Sinai Peninsula in Egypt, just beyond Israel's southern border. The victorious IDF forces in that conflict were commanded by Moshe Dayan. Rabin served as army chief of operations from 1959 to 1961 and as deputy chief of staff from 1961 until 1964, when he was named chief of staff of the IDF. By then, Levi Eshkol had succeeded Ben-Gurion as prime minister.

As IDF chief of staff, Rabin worked to improve Israel's military strength. He acquired warplanes, tanks, and more sophisticated weaponry from the United States. Rabin also favored the development of nuclear weapons as a deterrent. Rabin's biggest challenge and greatest success came in the spring of 1967. In May, Egyptian President Gamal Abdel Nasser closed the Strait of Tiran, leading into the Gulf of Aqaba, to Israeli shipping. This action blocked the Israeli port of Elat and cut off Israel's only access to the Red Sea. By June 5, Egypt had signed defense agreements with Syria, Jordan, and Iraq to create a joint military command. Fearing that an Arab attack was imminent, the Israelis decided to strike first. On June 5, Israel launched a surprise air attack against Egypt. Syria, Jordan, and Iraq immediately joined Egypt in the fighting. But within hours, the Israeli warplanes had destroyed nearly the entire Arab air forces. Israeli ground forces then went into action. IDF tanks rumbled into the Sinai Peninsula and captured it. The UN arranged a cease-fire that ended the war after six days. But by then, Israeli forces had taken over Syria's Golan Heights, an area bordering Israel to the north, and occupied two disputed territories: the West Bank, which had been claimed by Jordan, and the Gaza Strip, which had been controlled by Egypt. Israel vowed not to withdraw from the occupied territories until the Arab countries officially recognized Israel's right to exist. Rabin planned the strategy for the Six-Day War, as the Israelis later called it, and Dayan, the new minister of defense, made some prudent decisions that contributed to the war's outcome. Both men were hailed as military heroes. Dayan, already widely recognized for his leadership in the 1956 Arab-Israeli conflict, was accustomed to such public acclaim, but Rabin was not. However, he shyly enjoyed the attention, which also brought him a newfound respect that would help ease the way for his future career in politics.

Israeli Army Chief of Staff Rabin looks out the window on a flight over the Suez Canal region during the Sinai campaign of the Six-Day War in 1967.

Rabin retired from the Israel Defense Forces at the end of 1967. In 1968, Prime Minister Eshkol appointed him ambassador to the United States. Rabin arrived in Washington, D.C., in February. Leah and Yuval came with him, but Dalia, who was about to turn 18, stayed in Israel to graduate from high school and begin military service in the IDF. Yuval turned 13 later that year and had his *bar mitzvah,* a ceremony marking the entry of a Jewish boy into the adult Jewish community, at a synagogue in Washington, D.C. The Rabin family arrived at a turbulent time in American history. There were outbreaks of racial violence in reaction to the civil rights movement and protests against continued U.S. participation in the ongoing Vietnam War (1957–1975) that to the Rabins sometimes made peace seem as elusive in the United States as it was in Israel. But Ambassador Rabin worked with U.S. presidents Lyndon B. Johnson and Richard M. Nixon to strengthen diplomatic and political ties between the two nations. Back in Israel, Golda Meir became prime minister in 1969 following the death of Eshkol.

Rabin returned to Israel in the spring of 1973. He decided to run for a seat in the Knesset (Israel's parliament) as a candidate of the Labor Party. Under Israel's system of government, voters do not cast ballots for individual candidates to the Knesset. Instead, they select a party list that includes all candidates of a particular party. The number of seats each party gets is based on the proportion of the vote the party list received in the election. The leader of the party with the most Knesset seats usually is chosen prime minister. Rabin was placed on the Labor Party's list of candidates on Sept. 24, 1973. The election was scheduled for October, but an unexpected turn of events caused its postponement.

The Rabin family was at home on Oct. 5, 1973—the eve of Yom Kippur, the holiest day in Judaism—when a soldier arrived at the door with orders for Yuval to suspend his holiday leave and return immediately to the naval base where he was stationed. They were soon to learn why. On October 6, Egyptian and Syrian forces launched a full-scale attack on Israeli positions in the Sinai Peninsula and the Golan Heights. At first, the Israeli forces were driven out of these positions. However, in part because of Rabin's earlier efforts as ambassador to the United States, shipments of American military equipment soon arrived in Israel. By October 24, Israeli forces had crossed the Suez Canal and surrounded the Egyptian army in the south and recaptured the Golan Heights and some additional Syrian territory in the north. The United Nations called for a cease-fire, which went into effect on October 25. Although Rabin informally advised the chief of staff David Elazar during what became known in Israel as the Yom Kippur War, Rabin had no official role in the conflict.

The parliamentary elections finally were held on Dec. 31, 1973. The Labor Party held its majority, and Rabin won a seat in the Knesset. In March 1974, Prime Minister Meir appointed Rabin minister of labor.

FIRST TERM AS PRIME MINISTER

Although Israel won the Yom Kippur War, the country suffered heavy losses of personnel and equipment, and the expense of the conflict took a toll on the nation's economy. Many Israelis criticized the government's handling of the war. Meir announced her resignation as prime minister in early April 1974. On April 22, 1974, the Labor Party elected Rabin to succeed her. On June 3, 1974, Rabin took office as Israel's prime minister after a vote of approval by the Knesset. Rabin's government was formed from a fragile coalition of three parties—Labor, Independent Liberal, and Civil Rights Movement—that held a slim majority in the Knesset. Even within the Labor Party, which Rabin headed, there was much squabbling among the members over what direction the new government should take.

At age 52, Rabin was the youngest person at the time to become prime minister of Israel. He was also the first Israeli prime minister to be born in what is now Israel. All the previous prime ministers were born in Europe.

As prime minister, Rabin faced a variety of domestic and international issues. The domestic issues included problems with the

Rabin began his first term as prime minister of Israel on June 3, 1974. At age 52, he was the youngest person at the time to hold that title. Rabin is shown giving an address in 1974.

economy, such as inflation, and increased ethnic tensions between *Ashkenazic* and *Sephardic* Jews. Most Ashkenazic Jews are descendants of Jews from central and Eastern Europe. Sephardic Jews are descendants of Jews from Spain, Portugal, or other Mediterranean countries and the Middle East. Rabin also worked to rebuild the Israel Defense Forces.

In 1974 and 1975, Rabin worked closely with U.S. Secretary of State Henry Kissinger, who served as an intermediary in negotiating an agreement between Israel and Egypt for a disengagement of forces. Rabin five times met secretly with King Hussein I of Jordan in an attempt to open peace negotiations between their two nations, but these efforts were unsuccessful.

On June 27, 1976, while presiding over a cabinet meeting, Rabin received word that terrorists had hijacked an Air France plane en route from Tel Aviv to Paris. Many of the plane's passengers were Israeli citizens. After a stopover in Libya, the plane was directed to Entebbe Airport in Uganda the next day. The following afternoon, the hijackers demanded the release of 53 terrorists imprisoned in Israel and several other countries before they would give up their hostages on the plane. With the support of his cabinet, Rabin publicly agreed to conduct negotiations with the hijackers through the French government. However, he also instructed the IDF to devise a military operation to free the hostages. He took a brief break that evening to attend Dalia's graduation from law school and then returned to overseeing the crisis. On the afternoon of July 3, Rabin met with Defense Minister Shimon Peres and IDF military leaders to work out the details of the rescue plan that had been devised. Between 11:00 p.m. and midnight, Israeli commandos made a daring raid on the airport and saved 103 hostages. Three hostages and one Israeli ground commander died in the rescue operation—fewer casualties than expected given the risks of the mission. All the hijackers were killed. The overall success of the mission Rabin ordered once again made him a national hero.

On Feb. 22, 1977, opening day for the Labor Party's national convention preceding that year's parliamentary elections, Peres challenged Rabin for the position of party leader. On the second and final day of the convention, by a margin of only 41 votes, party delegates chose to keep Rabin as leader.

In March 1977, a newspaper reporter revealed the existence of an account in the names of Yitzhak and Leah Rabin at a bank in Washington, D.C., Israeli law prohibited Israeli citizens from maintaining bank accounts in another country without residing in that country. The Rabins had opened the account when they were living in Washington, D.C., while Yitzhak was ambassador to the United States. But Leah, who generally handled the couple's finances, failed to close the account when they returned to Israel and had withdrawn money from it several times afterward when visiting in the United States. The news broke when Leah finally attempted to close it during a visit earlier that month. Yitzhak vowed to share full responsibility for the violation with his wife, but they were charged separately. On April 7, Yitzhak was let off with a small fine, while Leah was scheduled to stand trial later in the month.

After Rabin was fined, he recorded a televised address in which he announced his resignation as prime minister and head of the Labor Party. On April 10, Peres was chosen to replace Rabin as the party's leader and candidate for prime minister in the upcoming parliamentary elections. At her trial on April 17, Leah Rabin was convicted of having an illegal bank account and fined 250,000 Israeli pounds (about $27,000). On May 17, Israeli voters cast their ballots for the Knesset. After 29 years as the opposition leader, the Likud bloc finally won the most seats. The Likud bloc, an alliance of several smaller groups, favored a more limited government role in the economy and a more hard-line policy toward Arab states. On June 21, Rabin officially handed over the office of prime minister to Likud leader Menachem Begin.

INTERIM POLITICAL ACTIVITIES

Although Rabin was no longer prime minister and Labor Party leader, he remained a member of the party and retained his seat in the Knesset. On Nov. 19, 1977, Rabin was among the Israeli dignitaries assembled in a receiving line at the airport in Jerusalem to welcome Egyptian President Anwar el-Sadat to Israel. Sadat had announced earlier that month that he was ready to negotiate a peace settlement with Israel. In their first brief face-to-face meeting, Rabin was impressed at Sadat's poise and diplomatic skill. The following afternoon, Rabin was impressed further when Sadat addressed the Knesset and expressed Egypt's desire to make peace with Israel even if none of the other Arab countries would. A series of talks arranged by U.S. President Jimmy Carter between Sadat and Begin led to the Camp David Accords. (The agreement was so called because the three men met at Camp David, the U.S. president's official retreat, located in Maryland, about 70 miles [113 kilometers] from Washington, D.C.) As a result of these accords, Egypt recognized Israel's right to exist, and Israel agreed to a phased withdrawal from the part of the Sinai Peninsula it still occupied. In March 1979, Egypt and Israel signed a peace treaty. Begin invited Rabin to join the Israeli delegation to witness the signing ceremony in Washington, D.C. Rabin included a description of these events in his autobiography, *The Rabin Memoirs*, published later that year.

At the Labor Party's national convention in December 1980, Rabin challenged Peres for the position of party leader but lost. In the parliamentary elections on June 30, 1981, the Likud bloc retained control of the Knesset, governing through a coalition that included smaller conservative parties. Later that year, Begin's government claimed legal and political authority over the Golan Heights. Syria and many other countries objected to this claim. In Egypt, Sadat was assassinated on Oct. 6, 1981, by a small group of Egyptian Islamic fundamentalists who opposed his policies. Rabin grieved the loss and worried about whether the peace with Egypt would last without that country's visionary leader. But Sadat's successor, Hosni Mubarak, continued Sadat's policies. In 1982, Israel completed its withdrawal from the Sinai Peninsula. Also that year, Israel invaded southern Lebanon and drove out guerrilla forces of the Palestine Liberation Organization (PLO), the political body that represents the Palestinian Arabs.

In September 1983, Begin resigned as prime minister. Likud member Yitzhak Shamir succeeded him. In the parliamentary elections held in July 1984, Labor won more seats than Likud, but neither party won a majority, and neither was able to form a coalition government. Thus, in September, the two parties agreed to form a unity government for 50 months. Under the agreement, Labor leader Peres would serve as prime minister for 25 months, with Likud leader Shamir serving as vice prime minister and foreign minister. In October 1986, after 25 months, the roles of Peres and Shamir would be reversed for the next 25 months. The unity government included cabinet members of both parties. On Sept. 13, 1984, Rabin was sworn in as minister of defense, a position he held until 1990.

In late 1987, Palestinian Arabs in the West Bank and Gaza Strip began an *intifada* (an Arabic word for *uprising*) against Israel's occupation of these territories. Some of the demonstrations were peaceful, but others became violent. Israeli soldiers killed a number of protesters during the violent demonstrations, and a few Israelis were also killed. Hundreds of Israelis and Palestinians were injured. As defense minister, Rabin was responsible for bringing the rioting under control. To reduce the number of deaths, he ordered Israeli soldiers to replace live ammunition with rubber bullets and water cannons. Later he authorized the use of "force, power, and blows"[1] in place of gunfire to break up demonstrations. But beating the rock-throwing protesters—some of whom were children—proved no more effective than shooting at them in stopping the demonstrations. Rabin realized that in the long run, the only solution would be a political rather than a military one. In May 1988, he began to meet secretly for talks with Palestinian leaders from the West Bank and Gaza Strip. In January 1989, he proposed a peace plan calling

In 1984, Rabin became minister of defense. He held this position until 1990. He is shown walking with Israeli troops in the West Bank in 1988.

for a six-month suspension of the intifada, during which time Palestinians in the occupied territories would elect representatives to negotiate an interim agreement with Israel. Both Shamir and the PLO—which in 1988 had recognized Israel's right to exist and declared its willingness to negotiate for peace with Israel in return for the establishment of an independent Palestinian state—rejected Rabin's plan.

The main difference between Rabin and Shamir regarding peace with the Palestinians centered on allocation of land. Rabin was willing to eventually concede some of the land in the occupied territories to the Palestinians to achieve peace. Shamir was not, and he also refused to negotiate with the PLO. In 1990, when Shamir continued to refuse to compromise on peace plans for the occupied territories, the Labor Party left the government coalition that had been formed after the November 1988 parliamentary elections in which neither Labor nor Likud won a majority. As a result, Shamir's government fell, but he formed a new government coalition a few months later with Likud and small conservative parties. Also in 1990, Rabin again challenged Peres for leadership of the Labor Party but again lost. However, Rabin finally succeeded in February 1992 and became head of the party.

PRIME MINISTER AND PEACEMAKER

Parliamentary elections in June 1992 brought the Labor Party to power, in part because of Rabin's reputation among Israelis as a strong leader who would protect the nation's security. In July, Rabin, replacing Shamir, again became prime minister. Rabin named himself minister of defense as well. He appointed Peres deputy prime minister and foreign minister. The two men put their personal differences aside to work toward their common goal of peace between Israel and the Palestinians. As a step toward this goal, Rabin agreed to limit construction of new Jewish settlements in the occupied territories.

Representatives of Israel and the PLO began secret peace talks in 1993. These negotiations took place mostly in or near Oslo, Norway, and produced two agreements known as the Oslo accords.

The first accord, officially known as the Declaration of Principles (DOP) but also called Oslo I, set up a framework and timetable for the peace process. It began a plan for self-government in the Gaza Strip and West Bank by calling for administration of the strip and the town of Jericho in the West Bank to pass from Israeli military forces to a new interim Palestinian government. Elections would eventually be held for a Palestinian Legislative Council. The PLO reiterated its recognition of Israel's right to exist, and Israel recognized the PLO as the representative of the Palestinian people. At the signing of Oslo I in Washington, D.C., on Sept. 13, 1993, Rabin publicly shook hands with PLO leader Yasir Arafat at a ceremony hosted by U.S. President Bill Clinton. Israel handed over control of Jericho and the Gaza Strip to the PLO in 1994. That year, the Palestinian Authority was created as the government for Palestinians in much of the West Bank and Gaza Strip. Rabin, Arafat, and Israeli foreign minister Peres shared the 1994 Nobel Peace Prize for their peace efforts.

U.S. President Bill Clinton, center, presides over ceremonies marking the signing of the Sept. 13, 1993, peace accord between Israel and the Palestinians on the White House lawn. Rabin, left, and PLO leader Yasir Arafat, right, shared the 1994 Nobel Peace Prize with Israeli foreign minister Shimon Peres for their peace efforts in the Middle East.

Rabin also worked to make peace with neighboring Arab countries. Since the mid-1970's, he had developed a close personal relationship with King Hussein I of Jordan. In October 1994, the two leaders signed a peace treaty to formally end the state of war that had technically existed between their two countries since 1948. The signing took place in the Arava Desert on the border between Israel and Jordan, with President Clinton in attendance.

On Sept. 28, 1995, Rabin and Arafat signed the Oslo II accord, formally called the Israeli-Palestinian Interim Agreement on the West Bank and the Gaza Strip, in Washington, D.C. Oslo II expanded on Oslo I with provisions for complete Israeli withdrawal from specified cities and towns in the West Bank. The agreement also set a timetable for elections for the Palestinian Legislative Council and detailed the powers of that body. Israel gave the Palestinians control of most West Bank cities and towns in 1995 and 1996.

ASSASSINATION AND LEGACY

Not all Israelis agreed with the peace process. Some who opposed it argued that Israel was giving away land that should historically belong to Israel. One of the people who opposed Rabin's policies was Yigal Amir, a right-wing (reactionary) Israeli university student. Amir organized campus demonstrations against Rabin's government, but soon his protest would take a more direct form.

On Nov. 4, 1995, Rabin addressed a peace rally in Tel Aviv. Many security measures were taken to prevent attacks by Arab terrorists, but little consideration was given to the possibility of a Jewish terrorist. Amir easily was able to mingle with the crowd of people leaving the rally. He lingered until Rabin descended the stairs from the speaker's platform and walked toward a waiting armored car, flanked on either side by bodyguards. Amir came up behind Rabin, pulled out the gun he had carried in his pocket, and shot the prime minister twice in the back. Rabin was rushed to a hospital, where surgeons made heroic efforts to save him, but the damage to his internal organs was too extensive. Leah Rabin, who had been nearby when the shooting occurred, was quickly placed into another car and eventually taken to the hospital, where she received the sad news that her husband had died.

Many world leaders attended Rabin's funeral. Amir later confessed to the murder. Peres became prime minister. As a result of the Oslo accords, Israeli forces withdrew from the Gaza Strip and part of the West Bank by 1996. Then in January 1996, Palestinians in these areas elected a legislature and a president. From 1996 to 2005, control of Israel's government shifted several times between Labor and Likud dominance, resulting in an inconsistency of leadership that hindered the peace process. Palestinians began a second intifada against Israel in September 2000. In 2002, Israel reoccupied most West Bank cities. But on Sept. 12, 2005, the last Israeli forces withdrew from the Gaza Strip, and the Palestinian Authority took control of the territory.

Rabin's family continued to carry on his legacy in various ways. His wife, Leah Rabin, published the memoir *Our Life, His Legacy* in 1997. Both their son, Yuval Rabin, and their oldest grandson, Jonathan Pelosoff, served in the Israel Defense Forces before Rabin's death, and their granddaughter, Noa Pelosoff, graduated from officers training school in October 1996. Their daughter, Dalia Rabin-Pelosoff, won a seat in the Knesset in the elections held in May 1999. She also has served as head of the administrative committee for the Yitzhak Rabin Center for Israel Studies in Tel Aviv. In addition to the center, many other public buildings in Israel and the United States have been named in Rabin's honor. ◼

Rabin was assassinated on Nov. 4, 1995, in Tel Aviv by a right-wing Israeli university student. Many world leaders attended Rabin's funeral.

Notes

DAVID BEN-GURION

1. David Ben-Gurion, *Memoirs* (New York: World Publishing Co., 1970) 38.
2. Ben-Gurion 34.
3. Michael Bar-Zohar, *Ben-Gurion: A Biography* (New York: Delacorte Press, 1978) 6.
4. Ben-Gurion 47.
5. Ben-Gurion 58.
6. Ben-Gurion 60.

GOLDA MEIR

Chapter 1
1. Golda Meir, *My Life* (New York: G. P. Putnam's Sons, 1975) 13–14.
2. Meir 38.
3. Meir 43.
4. Meir 52.
5. Meir 52.
6. Meir 61.
7. Meir 58.

Chapter 2
1. Meir 74.
2. Meir 88
3. Meir 97.
4. Meir 98–99.

Chapter 3
1. Meir 116–17.
2. David Ben-Gurion, *Israel: A Personal History* (Tel Aviv: American Israel Publishing Co., 1971) 54.
3. Meir 166.

4. Meir 187.
5. Meir 188–89.
6. Marie Syrkin, *Golda Meir: Woman with a Cause* (New York: G. P. Putnam's Sons, 1963) 141.
7. Meir 191.
8. Meir 191–92.
9. Meir 194.
10. Meir 200.
11. Qtd. in Syrkin 200.

Chapter 4
1. Meir 222.
2. Meir 222.
3. Meir 222.
4. Meir 226.
5. Meir 226–27.
6. Meir 228.
7. Meir 256.
8. Quoted in "A Tough, Maternal Legend," *Time*, 18 Dec, 1978: 43.
9. Meir 303–306.
10. Meir 348.
11. Meir 348.

Chapter 5
1. Meir 398.
2. Meir 423.
3. Meir 425.

YITZHAK RABIN

1. Robert Slater, *Rabin of Israel*. Rev. ed. (New York: St. Martin's Press, 1993) 338.

Recommended Reading

BOOKS

Ben-Gurion, David. *Memoirs*. New York: World Pub., 1970.

Gilbert, Martin. *Israel: A History*. New York: Morrow, 1998.

Horovitz, David P. *Shalom, Friend: The Life and Legacy of Yitzhak Rabin*. New York: Newmarket, 1996.

Kurzman, Dan. *Ben-Gurion: Prophet of Fire*. New York: Simon & Schuster, 1983.

—. *Soldier of Peace: The Life of Yitzhak Rabin, 1922–1995*. New York: HarperCollins, 1998.

Mann, Peggy. *Golda: The Life of Israel's Prime Minister*. New York: Coward, 1971.

Martin, Ralph G. *Golda: Golda Meir, the Romantic Years*. New York: Scribner, 1988.

Meir, Golda. *A Land of Our Own: An Oral Autobiography*. Ed. Marie Syrkin. New York: Putnam, 1973.

—. *My Life*. New York: Putnam, 1975.

Meir, Menachem. *My Mother, Golda Meir*. New York: Arbor Hse., 1983.

Rabin, Lea. *Rabin: Our Life, His Legacy*. New York: Putnam, 1997.

Rabin, Yitzhak. *The Rabin Memoirs*. Expanded ed. Berkeley: Univ. of Calif. Pr., 1996.

Reich, Bernard. *Historical Dictionary of Israel*. Metuchen, N.J.: Scarecrow, 1992.

—. and David H. Goldberg. *Political Dictionary of Israel*. Lanham, Md.: Scarecrow, 2000.

Slater, Robert. *Rabin of Israel*. New York: St. Martin's, 1993.

Teveth, Shabtai. *Ben-Gurion: The Burning Ground, 1886–1948*. Boston: Houghton, 1987.

—. *Ben-Gurion and the Palestinian Arabs: From Peace to War*. New York: Oxford, 1985.

WEB SITES

Israel Ministry of Foreign Affairs
<http://www.mfa.gov.il>

Jewish Virtual Library
<http://www.jewishvirtuallibrary.org>

The Knesset: The Israeli Parliament
<http://www.knesset.gov.il>

Yitzhak Rabin Center for Israel Studies
<http://www.rabincenter.org.il>

Glossary

aliyah *(ah lee YAH)* immigration to Israel by Jews.

anti-Semitism *(AN tee SEHM uh tihz uhm)* dislike or hatred for Jews; prejudice against Jews.

Ashkenazic *(ASH kuh NAZ ihk or AHSH kuh NAH zihk)* **Jew** a descendant of a member of a Jewish community of central and Eastern Europe.

Cossack *(KOS ak or KOS uhk)* one of a Slavic people living on the steppes in southwestern Russia, noted as horsemen and cavalrymen, especially in czarist Russia.

Diaspora *(dy AS puhr uh)* the scattering of the Jews after their captivity in Babylon; the parts of the world in which Jews live outside of Israel or, formerly, Palestine.

Haganah *(hah gah NAH)* an underground Jewish military organization in Palestine founded in 1920 and active until 1948.

heder *(khAY duhr or khEHD uhr)* an old type of Hebrew school that emphasized prayer and the study of the Bible and Talmud in Hebrew and Yiddish.

Holocaust *(HOL uh kawst)* the mass destruction or extermination of European Jews by the Nazis during World War II (1939–1945).

Judah *(JOO duh)* an ancient Hebrew kingdom in southern Palestine, made up of the tribes of Judah and Benjamin. Jerusalem was its capital.

kibbutz *(kih BOOTS)* an Israeli communal settlement, especially a farm cooperative.

Knesset *(KNEHS eht)* the Israeli parliament.

Messiah *(muh SY uh)* the leader and liberator of the Jews, promised by the prophets and looked for as the restorer of the theocracy.

Nazi *(NAHT see or NAT see)* a member or supporter of the National Socialist Party, a fascist political party in Germany, led by Adolf Hitler; advocate of Nazism. It came to power in Germany in 1933 and believed in state control of industry, denunciation of Communism and Judaism, and the dominance of Germany as a world power.

pogrom *(poh GROM or POH gruhm)* an organized massacre, especially of Jews.

prime minister the chief minister in certain governments, who is the head of the cabinet and the chief executive of the government.

Semite *(SEHM yt or SEE myt)* a member of the ancient and modern peoples speaking any of the Semitic languages. The ancient Hebrews, Phoenicians, and Assyrians were Semites. Arabs and Jews are sometimes called Semites.

Sephardic *(sih FAHR dihk)* **Jew** a descendant of a Jew from Spain, Portugal, or other Mediterranean countries and the Middle East.

socialism *(SOH shuh lihz uhm)* a theory or system of social organization by which the major means of production and distribution are owned, managed, or controlled by the government, by associations of workers, or by the community as a whole.

synagogue *(SIHN uh gawg or SIHN uh gog)* a building or place used by Jews for worship and religious instruction; temple.

yeshiva *(yuh SHEE vuh)* a Jewish school for higher education, often a rabbinical seminary; a Jewish elementary or high school in which both religious and secular subjects are taught.

Yiddish *(YIHD ihsh)* a language that developed from a dialect of German. Yiddish contains many Hebrew and Slavic words and is written in Hebrew characters. It is spoken mainly by Jews of eastern and central Europe and their descendants.

Zion *(ZY uhn)* a hill in Jerusalem on which the royal palace and the Temple stood; Israel or the Israelites; the people of Israel, whose national religious life centered on Mount Zion.

Zionism *(ZY uh nihz uhm)* a movement that started in the late 1800's to set up a Jewish national state in Palestine, and which now seeks to help maintain and develop the state of Israel.

Index

Page numbers in *italic* type refer to pictures.